Czech and Slovak Touches

Recipes

History, Travel, Folk Arts

The Czech Book *revised and expanded*

> "I am proud to be a descendant of both Czech and Slovak heritage. The commitment and hard work of both my maternal and paternal grandparents, as well as my mother and father, are typical of our culture and gave me the unique and special opportunities and privileges that I have enjoyed in my lifetime."
> — Captain Eugene Cernan
> Commander of Apollo XVII's venture to the moon
> Member, Board of Directors
> National Czech & Slovak Museum & Library

by Pat Martin

Penfield Press

Dedication

This revised and expanded edition of The Czech Book, is dedicated, once again, to the growing numbers of people of Czech, Moravian, and Slovak descent throughout North America, who contribute to our historic past and present. The preservation of this unique heritage is a gift to future generations of Americans.

About the author

Patricia A. Martin holds a B.A. degree in journalism and English education from Creighton University, Omaha, Nebraska, and a M.A. from the University of Iowa. A widow and mother of two sons, she is a language arts teacher and reading specialist.

As coordinator for the Cedar Rapids Czech Village Association, 1978–86, Pat's efforts have made significant contributions to the promotion and recognition of the Czech heritage community. She is the author of Penfield Press publications: *The Czech Book* (first edition of *Czech Touches*), *Czechoslovak Culture: Recipes, History and Folk Arts,* and *Czech Wit and Wisdom.*

Acknowledgements

In addition to the many contributors noted with their essays or recipes, we would like to thank Dan Baldwin, Director of the National Czech & Slovak Museum & Library; the Czech Village Association and its members; the Cedar Rapids, Iowa, community partners in the Czech Village Project; the Cedar Rapids and Iowa City public libraries; Marilyn Heise, Joyce Kramer, Laurie Lee, Rollie Raim, and Melvina Svec, all of Cedar Rapids; editors of *The Iowan* magazine; Mark Vasko-Bigaouette, St. Paul, Minnesota, director of Heritage Tours, and Olga Rychilikova of Prague, a tour guide for Heritage Tours.

Revised edition edited by: Dwayne and Joan Liffring-Zug Bourret,
    Dorothy Crum, and Melinda Bradnan
Graphic design by: Lance Lau and Walter Meyer

Front cover: Český Krumlov — Back cover: The Charles Bridge, Prague
Photographs by Joan Liffring Zug-Bourret

Books by mail (postpaid):
Czech Touches
    (this book), $16.95
Czech Culture
    by Pat Martin, $16.95

Czech Wit and Wisdom
    by Pat Martin, $10.95
Czech Proverbs
    by Joanne Asala, $14.85
Cherished Czech Recipes, $6.95

Penfield Press, 215 Brown Street, Iowa City, Iowa 52245

©1999 Penfield Press   ISBN 1-57216-029-2   Library of Congress #98-65713

Contents

Introduction: The Journey to Prague	4
The Czechs and Slovaks	
Two Republics Come of Age	5
Czech, Moravian and Slovak History	7
National Czech & Slovak Museum & Library	
Dedication	13
National Czech & Slovak Museum & Library	21
The Art of Living	25
Czech Pioneer Spirit	
Young Czech Weaver Stakes Free Land Claim	28
The Slovak from Cleveland	30
Czech Roots	33
Heritage Tours	34
CzechoSlovak Genealogical Society	34
Searching for Czech and Slovak Ancestry	35
Finding Ancestral Sites in the Czech Republic	36
Touring the Czech and Slovak Republics	
Prague	40
The Charles Bridge	44
Jewish Monuments	47
Český Krumlov	48
Strázňice	65
Peasant Baroque Architecture, Holašovice	67
Slovakian Showplaces	
Piešťany	68
Bratislava	70
Folk Arts and Lore	72
Traditional Celebrations	80
Czechs and Slovaks in America,	
Sites and Events	87
Among the Resources	93
Food for Thought in the Words of	
Czech Republic President Václav Havel	95
Recipes	97
Listing of Recipes	140

Introduction: A Dream Deferred —Then Realized
The Journey to Prague and the Two Republics

My Prague excursion occurred Summer, 1997, but the journey there began in my childhood. Growing up in Centerville, Iowa, I was always fascinated by the language, customs, foods and interests of a variety of ethnic groups, most of whom settled there to work in the McConville Coal Mines with my grandfather, his parents and brothers. Both sets of grandparents, the McConville coal miners and the Bradley bankers, settled in southern Iowa in the 1880s. Although my roots are Irish, my love of cultural diversity embraced a number of ethnics, and I especially recall Czech, Slovak, and Yugoslav heritage. I thought every place in the world enjoyed the wealth of cultural heritage that we shared in my hometown.

During my high school years, I enjoyed performances of folk dancing and music. I loved the music of Antonín Dvořák and wanted to go to Czechoslovakia, especially Prague, but that would have to wait until I was financially independent!

In 1964, I moved to Cedar Rapids, Iowa, to begin my first teaching job in southwest Cedar Rapids, a predominantly Czech neighborhood. During this time, in 1971, the Czechs had the estimated high concentration of some 30 percent of the population of Linn County, Iowa. Several events established a resurgence in Czech pride in the community. The Czech Village Association began to organize for redevelopment and renovation of that historical area. Much to my delight, they recruited me to coordinate their project.

In 1994, I began to write a book about the Charles Bridge in Prague, long a source of fascination to me. As I talked about the book, my sister said, "Patty, you are not going to publish another book about the Czech culture without going there. We will both go next summer!" So, we went!

"The Eternal City"..."The Golden City"..."City of Seven Hills" ... "City of 1000 Spires." It's all true! Prague is as endearing as these descriptions. A trip to fulfill a dream—but most importantly, it substantiated my kindred spirit with the Czech and Slovak culture. This revision of *The Czech Book,* is an outgrowth of that 1997 visit.

—*Pat Martin*

The Czechs and Slovaks
Two Republics Come of Age

A brief perspective on common history and events leading to the amiable separation.

The Czech and Slovak Republics lie snugly side-by-side in the heart of Europe. Throughout history the Czechs and Slovaks, like allied siblings, have shared common history and traditions. However, despite many similiarities, they were too different to live together in political and economic harmony and have parted amiably.

There is archaeological evidence of habitation of these lands from prehistoric times. One of the Celtic tribes, the Boii, gave the part of the Czech Republic known as Bohemia its name. The Celts were driven out by Germanic tribes towards the end of the fourth century A.D. The first Slavs, predecessors of the present population of the Czech and Slovak Republics, arrived in the fifth century. By the ninth century the Slav tribes had united to form the Great Moravian Empire, which included Bohemia, Moravia, Slovakia, and part of Austria. Despite common Slavic roots and cultural similiarities, after the collapse of the Great Moravian Empire at the beginning of the tenth century, the two countries came of age in two entirely different geo-political neighborhoods.

The geographical distinction of being in the heart of Europe was an asset for political and economic accessibility. A major advantage was the cultural stimulus the area enjoyed as the crossroads of Europe. This geographical distinction was also a massive burden. First, the countries are landlocked. Further, the two countries combined are no larger than New York State or England. With the military disadvantages of a small nation, they were unable to defend themselves against conquerors who coveted the mineral riches of Bohemia, the fertile farmlands of Slovakia, and the trade route their strategic location established.

For the next 1,000 years after the collapse of the Great Moravian Empire, both countries were mostly under the thumb of others. The

Holy Roman Empire and Hapsburg dynasty ruled the Czechs while the Hungarian Empire ruled the Slovaks. When the new country of Czechoslovakia emerged at the end of World War I, two countries that had lived in close proximity to one another realized that they were quite different.

A separate Slovak consciousness began to develop in the 1800s, but efforts to promote national identity were undermined by the Hungarian monarchy. Likewise the Czechs had been weakened by conquering nationals for centuries and struggled to maintain their language and culture. The Czechs' sense of National Revival began in the early 1800s, as well. Slovakia was primarily agricultural, while Bohemia and Moravia, the Czech lands, had an industrial heritage. There were even differences in the languages.

In 1918, the Allies created the Czecho-Slovak Republic. The nation was troubled from the start; Slovakia was somewhat more of a province than an equal partner. The Republic's position was precarious because of Nazi Germany's claims and invasion on the territories. Next, following World War II in 1948, the Soviet troops took over and a Communist regime ensued.

January 1, 1993, three years after the violence free Velvet Revolution in Czechoslovakia formalized the failure of communism, the Czechs and Slovaks went their independent ways as the Czech and Slovak Republics. Still today, however, both nations are united in numerous ways. They are bound together by families, friendships, history and tradition, as well as by the horrors of World War II and the fears and frustrations of living together throughout the Communist era. They also share the joy of the peaceful Velvet Revolution.

Together the Republics form a stronghold of magnificent history. From the skyline of the Golden City of Prague, to the pastoral scenes of Moravian wine country, to the hiking, mountain climbing, and skiing delights of the High Tatra Mountains in Slovakia, these two Republics are a tourist delight! And everywhere, there are ancient castles and churches, lush river valleys, glacial lakes, waterfalls, and music, dancing, and folk festivals.

Czech, Moravian, and Slovak History

Some Significant Dates

A.D. 500
 The Romans named Bohemia after the Alpine Boii Tribe living there. The Czechs migrated from the Vistula River to Central Europe. According to legend, they were guided there by Čechus or Čech, their chieftain.

623
 Frankish merchant Samo organized the Slavic tribes into a kingdom centered in Bohemia.

813–33
 At the end of the 8th century, there were two princedoms on the territory of Slovakia, Pribina's in Nitra and Mojmir's in Western Slovakia and Southern Moravia. In the years 813 to 833, the princedoms united and laid the foundation of the Great Moravian Empire.

862–63
 Cyril and Methodius brought Christianity to Moravia. Part of their missionary work was accomplished in their creation of a Slav alphabet, an accomplishment that ensured a literary culture for these people.

870–94
 Great Moravia began to flourish under Prince Svatopluk.

907
 The Magyars invaded Slovakia, ending the period of the Great Moravian Empire. The Slovak and Czech lands (Bohemia and Moravia) began periods of domination by different political forces.

929
 Prince Wenceslas was murdered by his brother and became the patron saint of Bohemia.

965
 The Jewish merchant Abraham Ben Jacob wrote the first description of the city of Prague, "built of stone and limestone," and termed it the "largest trading city in those lands."

1100–1400
 The Holy Roman Empire invited German merchants, artisans, and miners to settle in Bohemia and Slovakia. From A.D. 500 to 1620, there were wars with German and Magyar invaders.
  1140–72
   Prince Vladislav II became King Vladislav I in 1158. He directed the building of "Judith Bridge," the first stone bridge across the River Vltava.
  1346–78
   King Charles reigned and Prague experienced its most glittering Golden Age, becoming the largest city in Central Europe.
  1348
   Charles University, the first university in central Europe was founded in Prague.
  1357
   The foundation for the famous Charles Bridge, replacing the "Judith Bridge," was laid. Completed in 1399, the bridge is still standing today.
1415
 Jan Hus, Bohemian religious reformer, was burned at the stake. This execution touched off decades of religious and ethnic warfare in Central Europe.
1419–36
 The Hussite Wars and the First Defenestration of Prague. Touched off by Hus's death, rebellious Hussites, led by Jan Žižka, initiated decades of religious and ethnic warfare when several councillors were thrown from the window of the New Town Hall in Prague. Many German Catholics fled Bohemia.
1467
 Comenius University of Bratislava, the oldest university in Slovakia, was founded.
1576–1612
 Emperor Rudolph II's reign gives Prague a second Golden Age. Important European artists and scientists worked for the king. Protestant groups joined the Lutherans and drew up the *Confessio Bohemia*, officially the "Letter of Majesty of Rudolph II."

1618–48
> The Second Defenestration of Prague precipitated the Bohemian War which later developed into the Thirty Years' War. In accordance with old Bohemian custom, two of the emperor's men and their secretary were thrown from a Council room window at Hradčany (Prague Castle), May 23, 1618, due to supposed violations of religious issues cited in the "Letter of Majesty."

1620, November 8
> The Czechs were defeated by the Hapsburgs in the battle of White Mountain. The Czech crown lands were no longer independent. Thirty-six thousand families fled into exile.

1633
> Augustine Herrman, the first Czech immigrant arrived in America.

1740
> Maria Theresa became the Hapsburg empress. Under her more liberal regime, Catholic control of education lessened and Czech culture began to revive.

1741
> Groups of Moravian Brethren begin to arrive in America, settling in Pennsylvania, North Carolina and Georgia.

1848
> Revolts broke out in many European capitals, including Prague and Vienna. The Hapsburgs of Austria gained greater control. The Czechs lived under a system of semi-serfdom with the Austrian lords holding the most valuable land. Czech peasant families lived on small plots.

1860–1911
> Czech peasants paid redemption fees, sold possessions and came to America for cheap land. The lure of the California gold rush mixed with failure of potato crops, floods and droughts brought waves of Czech immigrants to America. Approximately 326 Czech newspapers flourished in America.

1866
> The first Czech bank was established in Chicago. A con-

stant flow of Czechs settled in Illinois, Iowa, Minnesota, Nebraska, Ohio, Wisconsin and Texas.

1882
Large groups of Slovaks begin to emigrate to America, settling in the industrial regions of Pennsylvania and Ohio.

1900–1910
Large scale Slovak immigration to America.

1914–18
Czechs and Slovaks living abroad joined Czechs and Slovaks and other national groups of Austria-Hungary in their campaign for an independent state leading to the new Republic of Czechoslovakia.

1918, October 28
The Bill of Rights for the Republic of Czechoslovakia was signed in the historic town hall of Philadelphia, Pennsylvania, site of the signing of the United States Declaration of Independence. Tomáš G. Masaryk was elected the first president of Czechoslovakia. One of U.S. President Woodrow Wilson's Fourteen Points called for the self-determination of minorities in Central Europe based on ethnic and language considerations. This doctrine and the defeat of Germany in World War I made possible the founding of a free Czechoslovakia.

1920–1930
Many Czechs emigrated to the United States. Cedar Rapids, Iowa, became noted for having the largest population of Czechs per capita, with over one-fourth of the residents of Czech descent.

1933
Adolph Hitler rose to power in Germany and called for the 3.5 million ethnic Germans living in the Sudeten district of Czechoslovakia to have autonomy.

1935
Eduard Benés was elected the second president of Czechoslovakia. During World War II, his government was in exile in London, England.

1938
  Neville Chamberlain, Prime Minister of Great Britain, in an agreement with France, gave in to Hitler's territorial demands for the Sudetenland. Hungary seized the Magyar area of Southern Slovakia and Poland took the city of Teschen.

1939
  The Germans helped create a puppet republic in Slovakia and turned Bohemia and Moravia into a protectorate. Hungary absorbed Ruthenia.

1945, May
  The provisional government of Benés returned to Prague at the end of the war. Ruthenia was conceded to the Ukraine due to language and ethnic similarities of the people. Slovakia was granted autonomy within the Republic, and expulsion of the Germans began.

1946, May
  In an election, the Communists received 38 percent of the vote, more than any other political party in Czechoslovakia.

1948, February
  Communist coup d'etat. The Communists took control of Czechoslovakia's government, and a new constitution was drafted. Ján Masaryk, son of Tomáš Masaryk, plunged to his death from a palace window in Prague. It is still not known if his death was a murder or suicide, but it awakened America to the dangers of expanding Communism.

1948, June
  President Benés resigned. Klement Gottwald, Communist party leader, became president. Czechoslovakia was renamed a "People's Democratic Republic." The government began collectivization of farm land and businesses.

1968, January
  Alexander Dubček, a Slovak, became general secretary of the Czechoslovak Communist Party, lifting censorship and giving more freedom of religion and of the press, promising increased independence for Slovakia. This brief period of liberalization was known as the "Prague Spring."

1968, August
Troops from the Soviet Union, Bulgaria, East Germany, Hungary and Poland invaded Czechoslovakia to resist the era of the Prague Spring, or the humanization of socialism.

1975
Charter 77, a declaration to protest then president Gustav Husak's harsh policies was advanced by an emerging organization demanding greater freedom and independence. Their leader, playwright Václav Havel and future president, was imprisoned along with other signers of the document.

1989–90
Czechoslovakia was one of the last Central European countries to take advantage of new liberal possibilities created by Soviet President Mikhail Gorbachev. Mass demonstrations and a general strike in November-December, 1989, led to the peaceful Velvet Revolution. The existing government resigned and a democratic multi-party system was introduced with the repeal of the Communist Party's right of control. Dissident playwright Václav Havel became president. Country's name was changed to Czech and Slovak Federal Republic. Vladimir Meciar became leader of the largest political party in Slovakia.

1992
In June elections, Václav Klaus wins majority in Bohemia and Moravia. On July 17, Slovakia declares independence. President Havel resigns from office. Negotiations for division of Slovak and Czech lands are completed by December.

1993, January 1
Czech and Slovak Republics become independent, sovereign states. Václav Havel was elected President of the Czech Republic and Michael Kováč was elected the first president of the Slovak Republic.

National Czech & Slovak Museum & Library Dedication

October 21, 1995

Presidents
Václav Havel, Czech Republic
Michal Kováč, Slovak Republic
William Jefferson Clinton, United States of America

Excerpts in the order presented:

Václav Havel
President of the Czech Republic

"Dear Presidents, Mr. Governor, Senators and Congressmen, ladies and gentlemen. I hope you will excuse me for speaking in Czech, but I really do think that the occasion warrants it.

"When I traveled here to Cedar Rapids and pondered upon the meaning of this trip, I thought, among other things, of a small train station not far away from Prague, and a small train station not far away from here. I recalled the fate of a man who, 100 years ago, made the journey between these two places, and I thought of the music which accompanied him as he went.

"Some of you may have guessed that the stations are those of Nehalozeves in the vicinity of Prague, and of Spillville, Iowa; the man I am talking about is Antonín Dvořák, and the music, the Czech and American melodies which were the background for the unique "New World Symphony." Antonín Dvořák, as you know well, was neither the first nor the last Czech to undertake this kind of a journey. At first hundreds, and later thousands and tens of thousands of Czech feet were treading the same pass from the heart of Europe to the harbors on the East Coast of the United States. From there to the center of the Midwest....Many of our fellow countrymen eventually settled here in Cedar Rapids. They came here to Iowa to find here freedom, prosperity and mutual tolerance. It was here that they felt that "this is the land" which, as I have been told, is the original Indian meaning of the word Iowa....

"During the 100 years which have passed since Dvořák's visit to Iowa, the people in which the local Czech settlers have their roots have gone a long way as well. It was a journey in time rather than in space, but the goals were the same—freedom, tolerance and prosperity.

"After decades of oppression and absence of freedom, we have now reached a situation when we, too, can say in our home, 'this is the land.' It seems that our respective pasts have brought us to the same or, at least, a similar point. We are united by the same ideals. We believe in the same values, and we share the desire to cherish and protect them. Our experience, often a bitter one, has taught us that they cannot be simply taken for granted as something 'that will just be there forever, even if we were to do nothing for it.'

"Perhaps this fact is best expressed in the motto of the state of Iowa: 'Our liberties we prize, and our rights we will maintain.' It is these words that guided the steps of the Czech travelers here to Iowa. They might as well have guided our own steps on our own journey. Thank you."

Michal Kováč
President of the Slovak Republic

"Mr. President Clinton, Mr. President Havel, dear compatriots, distinguished guests: It is partly symbolic that three presidents meet in the museum of American Czechs and Slovaks. Presidents of the countries, which in spite of a number of differences, do share a lot. We share our common struggle for democracy and humanity, and also the fact that two small Central European nations have long-lasting, positive relations to the United States, where part of their history took place.

"Thanks to this unique historic experience of our nations, we can speak of our good relations as something natural.

"Many Slovaks found their new home in the American continent in the most difficult times of our not distant history. They came in three big waves — first to seek work, later because of their resistance against the Communist dictatorship, and, at last, they escaped in front of the tanks of the Warsaw Pact armies, which tried to suffocate the democratic spirit in Central Europe.

"Most of our compatriots, who were chased to the world in thousands, found open arms here in the United States. Our countrymen were always good American patriots, and they actively participated in the flourishing development of their new homeland. But... American Slovaks have crucially realized the necessity to free the nation (Slovakia) from Hungarian oppression and they signed important agreements in Pittsburgh and Cleveland together with the Czech political representatives on the establishment of a new state, Czecho-Slovakia....

"The Slovak Republic and the Czech Republic, states of very close nations, arose from the common state in a peaceful way, by negotiations. I am proud of this positive historic precedence. Therefore, I am convinced that the Czech and Slovak communities abroad, and especially here in the United States, will follow this precedence, and they will find enough reasons for mutual dialogue, for cooperation in reaching our mutual goals while respecting all differences....

"The Slovak Republic is returning to where it culturally and historically belongs—to the world of democracy and prosperity. Therefore we are glad that, along with good Czech-Slovak relations, we can follow also the deep traditions of Slovak-American relations. This is our national contribution to stability in Central Europe for which we are prepared to do our utmost to send signals of peace and stability to our space.

"The National Czech & Slovak Museum has embraced positive examples from the past. I am convinced that we, today's politicians, as well as our successors, will not write the pages of our common history in dark colors.

"This moment, the meeting of the presidents of the three countries, could be one of the prerequisites confirming that our nations are ready to come with a new contribution to the treasury of our common history. I wish that this contribution brings benefit to all of us equally: the Slovaks, the Czechs, the Americans as well as to the nations of Europe. Thank you for your attention."

William Jefferson Clinton
President of the United States of America

"...I am proud to stand here with these two presidents, each a pioneer and a patriot, each leading his nation through an epic transformation, each representing the promise of Europe's future, and their presence today reflects our growing partnership as well as the deep roots of their people in the soil of Iowa....

"In his devotion to democracy and through his courage and sacrifice, Václav Havel helped to make the dreams (democracy) of those young people a reality. And the world is in his debt.

"President Kováč stands with us as the leader of a newly independent nation with a proud heritage and a hopeful future. Mr. President, we know your job has been and continues to be difficult, and the United States supports your personal strong commitment to openness and reform as Slovakia takes its place within the family of democratic nations. And we thank you for your leadership...."

Lion on the Bridge of Lions, Cedar Rapids, Iowa, crossing the river to the National Czech & Slovak Museum & Library. The lion statues are a gift from the Czech Heritage Foundation.

Three presidents attended the dedication of the National Czech & Slovak Museum & Library in October, 1995. From left: Slovak Republic President Michal Kováč, U.S. President William Jefferson Clinton, and Czech Republic President Václav Havel.

The National Czech & Slovak Museum & Library
Cedar Rapids, Iowa

John Johnson photographs

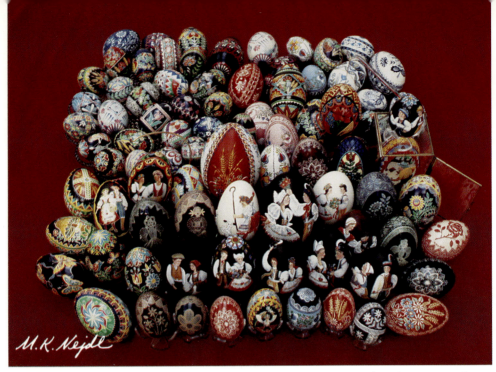

Decorated eggs are by folk artist Marj Nejdl, Cedar Rapids. Marj has demonstrated *kraslice* (egg decorating) at the Smithsonian Institute in Washington, D.C.

Czech, Moravian, and Slovak Americans wear their beautiful *kroje* in the Roman L. Hruska Grand Hall of the National Czech & Slovak Museum & Library. Mark Vasko-Bigaouette, of Heritage Tours, is standing fourth from the left.

Joan Liffring-Zug Bourret photos

Daniela Sipkova-Mahoney of Portland, Oregon, in a century old Moravian costume, holds a basket of eggs she has decorated.

Joan Liffring-Zug Bourret photo

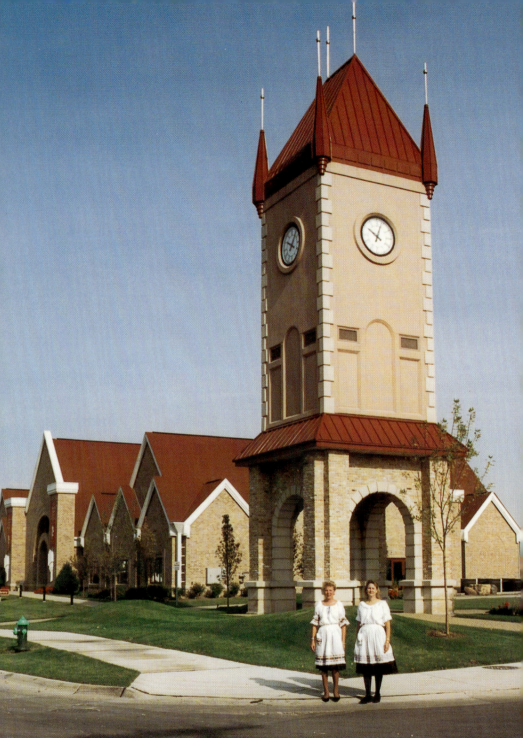

Chris Barta Jones and her sister Nancy Barta, owners of a family business in the Czech Village, Cedar Rapids, Iowa, stand by the Clock Tower of the National Czech & Slovak Museum & Library.

Joan Liffring-Zug Bourret photograph

National Czech & Slovak Museum & Library

Cedar Rapids, Iowa

Presiding over the Past, Present, and Future

Pride, partnership and perseverance led to the establishment of the new 18,000-square-foot National Czech & Slovak Museum & Library, Cedar Rapids, Iowa. The Czech and Slovak cultures were carefully preserved within private homes and families, fraternal organizations, and churches since the Czechs and Slovaks first settled in the Cedar Rapids, Iowa, area in the 1850s. Today, more than 5,000 artifacts, items as old as 400 years, nearly fifty elaborate *kroje* (national folk costumes) representing the Czech, Moravian, and Slovakian regions, and much more form the permanent collection of this Museum. The collection presents an extravagantly beautiful, rich, and authentic corridor to the past of our Western civilization. That corridor has been visited to date by Museum guests from more than seventy countries.

The Museum was dedicated in October, 1995, with a grand fanfare that included United States President Bill Clinton, President Václav Havel of the Czech Republic, and President Michal Kováč of the Slovak Republic. Dignitaries included Madeleine Albright, who has since become U.S. Secretary of State, and many others who joined in the dedication ceremony that praised a community that has consistently invested its time, talent, and treasure to celebrate its peoples' history.

The first Czech arrived in Linn County in about 1850, according to written documentation penned in 1855, by a settler named Thomas Korab. Czechs, Slovaks and Moravians stayed mostly in Johnson and Linn Counties, where they homesteaded farms or migrated to the shores of the Cedar River that provided a source of food, ice, and transportation.

The earliest settlers on the Cedar River started their own businesses to support their needs, resuming Old Country crafts and trades. The first major settlement of Czechs and Slovaks was on the southeast side of Cedar Rapids. When barge traffic became too heavy, a bridge was built to connect the two sides of the area. The area of businesses that comprise Czech Village today was founded.

It was not until the 1972 establishment of the Czech Village Foundation, however, that the first proactive preservation efforts for Czechoslovak culture occurred in the Cedar Rapids area. Two years later, in 1974, the Czech Heritage Foundation was organized. From this group, the Czech Fine Arts Foundation was born.

In 1978 the Czech Fine Arts group established the first museum, called the Czech Museum and Library, located in a small, wood-frame house near the corner of 16th Avenue and C Street S.W. Museum founders, all members of the Czech Fine Arts Foundation, knew they had to have a place to display, and that little house was a beginning.

Training for guides was held, and workshops on artifacts were conducted; goals and objectives were written. In 1980 the Foundation acquired a 30x60-square-foot block building on the west bank of the Cedar River in Czech Village for the second Museum site. Promotion of the Czech Village and museum has been active and on-going with continual Czech festivals, museum events and workshops featuring Old World arts, crafts, and artifacts.

Today, some 150 years after the first Czechs settled in this area, the National Czech & Slovak Museum & Library is located on the eastern border of Czech Village. The Village is one of Iowa's most distinctive ethnic enclaves, where authentic Czech food is available and where Czech culture remains vibrant.

The Museum, however, does more than spotlight Old World influences and continued interest in and appreciation of the local cultural heritage. This showcase is also an expression of the importance of the Czech and Slovak culture to the culture of the world. Planning and overseeing are dedicated to upgrading and increasing exhibits, developing a library that supports research utilization of the some 10,000 volumes in the Czech and Slovak languages, and continued programming of a gem of an immigrant home sited on Museum property.

The Museum's regard for the highest quality programming was evident in an extraordinary exposition staged in the facility May, 1997 to January, 1998. "A Thousand Years of Czech Culture: Riches from the National Museum in Prague" displayed some 203 artifacts of grand historic significance and beauty. These artifacts and works of art traced the remarkable history and cultural achievements of the Czech people.

Whatever the ethnic backgrounds of the some 30 thousand guests who viewed the collection, this exhibit, displaying the development of one of the world's great cultures, was a gratifying, inspirational adventure. People from all 50 states and 39 foreign countries visited the exhibition.

That exhibition spurred important donations to the Museum's permanent exhibit that opened on April 30, 1998. "Homelands: The Story of the Czech & Slovak People" is a multi-media exploration of the lives, celebrations, and travails of these European peoples. This long-awaited permanent exhibition provides artifacts from, and insight into the lives of the ancient peoples, from the days of the Slavic tribes wandering into Central Europe through the Velvet Divorce of 1993. Sections of "Homelands," such as "Arts and Letters," "Three Struggles for Freedom," and "Immigration and Acculturation" profile historic figures, artistic achievements, and the political accomplishments of the Czechs and Slovaks. A center of the new exhibition is "Costume Square," featuring some of the Museum's extensive *kroje* collection displayed in front of dramatic images appropriate to each region: Bohemia, Moravia, and Slovakia.

Because the Museum's entire and vast collection is not all on display simultaneously in this exhibition, other costumes and artifacts are rotated into the "Homelands" exposition, adding a dimension of renewed energy and freshness to the exhibit's permanency. "Homelands" is appealing to visitors of all ages. A large "castle," reminiscent of a medieval structure, is a major staging area as guests enter the first thematic section of the exhibit. A Czech language program provides audible Czech pronunciations of English words typed into a computer.

Antique pipes and doll collections, lavish laces, lead crystal, and ancestral paintings are displayed along with traditional painted eggs, colorful glassware, porcelain and ceramic objects, and woodcarvings.

A Mucha print, rare maps, a printing press on which Czech-language newspapers were printed, a bust of Stefanik, and a 1935 Czech-made motorcycle, an extensive stamp collection, and an Albin Polacek sculpture from the Art Institute in Chicago were on display for the first time in this exhibit.

The library of the Museum contains historic newspapers as well as the large collection of books, many in the Czech and Slovak languages. Subjects include geography, history, cookbooks, and novels. Museum officials hope to extend the collection to books of similar content but written in English. A non-circulating research library, much of this collection has been developed through donations, which are still accepted.

On-going educational programming at the Museum includes folk crafts, seminars, lectures, travelogues, folk and classical music concerts, tours for school children, and a variety of temporary exhibits. *(See section "Among Resources" for information.)*

The National Czech & Slovak Museum & Library is an ornament, not only to the Cedar Rapids area, but to Iowa as well. It also provides an opportunity to establish a legacy for generations. Notably in 1998, an exquisite chandelier, created in the Czech Republic, was installed in the Roman L. Hruska Grand Hall. This elegant and traditionally Czech and Slovak piece of decorative art was funded by Leora Zahorik and Edwin V. Zahorik, Jr. and dedicated in memory of their parents.

Willard A. Boyd, Professor of Law at the University of Iowa and President Emeritus of the Field Museum and the University of Iowa, stated: "The National Czech & Slovak Museum & Library will be a center where visitors of diverse cultural backgrounds can appreciate their common concerns and develop mutual respect for each other." — Professor Boyd is a member of the Museum Board of Directors.

The Art of Living

Music, dance, objects of beauty, literature and the mastering of crafts or skills—all are a part of "The Art of Living." These arts abound in the lives of Americans of Czech and Slovak heritage. There is a Czech folk custom testifying to the importance of the arts in the hearts and minds of the Czech people. "A baby, when first interested in exploring objects around him, was offered a coin and a violin. If he chose the violin, he would become a musician and if he chose the coin, it was predicted that he would become a thief."

Before the Czech and Slovak families began emigrating to the United States in the early 1850s, they lived in a state of semi-serfdom in Bohemia. For more than 200 years before the 1850s, Austrian lords owned the most valuable land while the Czechs held small pieces of undesirable land. In those days music was a profession that enabled them to rise above their circumstances. Accomplishments in the arts allowed one to accomplish something monetarily and to "become someone."

Without an art to elevate one, a person might never hope to attain anything beyond the simple peasant life. Further, even if an accomplished artist did not make a living from one of the arts, the mastering of the art would set the artist apart from, say, another tradesman or craftsman or farmer who had not mastered an art. To perform a task, the lords would hire the person who had a local reputation as an artist instead of hiring someone with fewer accomplishments.

So, art was much more than an injection of beauty and delight into the artist's world. It was an element of survival. The Czech people knew that skill in art could ensure success for future generations.

The Czech people are an ancient people, descendants of Slavic tribes first shown in the records in the fifth century. Theirs has been a history of struggling to preserve their heritage, because it has been also a history of struggling against invasions of foreigners—outsiders who wanted Czech land and natural resources. The culmination of their struggle against invasions came with the Czech defeat by the Hapsburgs in the Battle of White Mountain, outside of Prague, in 1620. This battle ended the Czech crown lands' independence as a nation and, as a result, some 36,000 families eventually went into exile, choosing anywhere, including America, over the semi-serfdom rule of the Hapsburgs.

The first Czechs came to America in 1633. Many of these immigrants were farmers and were poor. Others had uncommon skills derived from a rich and ancient culture. For example, the first university in Central Europe was established in Prague 100 years before Columbus discovered America.

Czechs brought with them to America the first lawyer to settle west of the Mississippi, Joseph Sosel. A young lawyer who had taken part in a Prague uprising, he escaped from Czechoslovakia by being rolled across the border in a barrel. In Cedar Rapids, Iowa, he learned English and taught others, and the new Czech community quickly stabilized. Sosel's daughters, Josephine and Mary, were principals of Cedar Rapids grade schools in the early 1900s.

The soul of a Czech has always found a voice in his music. In Bedřich Smetana, Czech music became an outlet for national feeling as well as the deeper emotions of the heart of the people—love of country, enjoyment of its beauties. "The Bartered Bride," an opera first produced in Prague in 1866, is still popular today in America. Another Czech, Antonín Dvořák, was inspired to complete his "New World Symphony" while living in Spillville, Iowa. This is a beautiful little Czech village on the banks of a river with a mill and a very large fieldstone Catholic church.

The Czech immigrants were inclined to be clannish. They lived near Czech tradesmen, Czech banks, Czech theatres and Czech stores. Fraternal organizations and clubs have long been important to Czechs. Through these groups, the heritage of the Czech people in America has been nurtured over the past 130 years. Many organized quilting and sewing groups still meet weekly and help ensure the continuation of traditional arts.

Some Czech and Slovak women retain the old country "dracky," or feather stripping party, if only in a modified form. Geese are not easily come by these days! Feather stripping involves the sorting of goose feathers, separating the fine down from the

Early twentieth-century kitchen in an immigrant home is displayed at the National Czech & Slovak Museum & Library, Cedar Rapids.

quills. At Czech festivals, Viki Polehna has demonstrated the making of *"pirkas,"* or feather basters, using only the seven or eight rounded feathers from the bottom of each wing. Viki considers a *"pirka"* as just another kitchen tool, but it exemplifies an ethnic custom of charm and importance.

Czechs have always painted and decorated ornate eggs during the Easter season. As a child, Cedar Rapids, Iowa artist Marj Nejdl "thought that everybody spent hours and hours decorating eggs at this season." Her work, includes batik, or wax resist decorating, and handpainted and pen and ink designs and scenes.

Physical fitness is also an art to the Czech people, and many Czechs credit the Sokol movement with making the most vital contribution toward fostering Czech heritage while also being a school for American democracy. The aim of the Sokols (Falcons) is a strong mind in a strong body.

Festivals displaying arts and culture are held throughout the United States. The Czech and Slovak people left behind them a land which knew a grand history and culture. Throughout generations of war and oppression in Europe, they maintained their heritage and brought that heritage, their music, arts and customs to their new country. Throughout America, this heritage is being kept alive to reinvigorate today and to give confidence for tomorrow.

Czech Pioneer Spirit
Young Czech Weaver Stakes Free Land Claim, the Cherokee Run
As told by Vlasta Skalnik Kolarik, Caldwell, Kansas

Excerpts from a story submitted to a Sumner County Fair Cherokee Strip Story Contest. Provided by her daughter, Anna Petrik, Caldwell, Kansas.

My father, Jehn Skalnik, a weaver by trade, came to America from Kardesova Recice, Czechoslovakia in 1888—the year of the great blizzard. His girlfriend, Frances, from the same city, came a year later. Not wishing to make the long journey alone, she asked her friend, Antonia Konopicka, also from the same city, to come with her....As often happens, the young lovers quarreled, my father transferred his affections to Antonia, and on May 24, 1890, they were married at Wilber, Nebraska.

They started housekeeping on a farm near Reynolds, Nebraska, and a few years later moved to Mahaska, Kansas, where father got a job working on the railroad. By this time, they had two children....In September, 1893, Father left...in the company of two friends, Frank Koran and Vaclav Melka...They came to Caldwell the day before the Cherokee Strip Opening. That night they slept under the open sky somewhere in our city. Caldwell was crowded with thousands of men and women, horses, and every imaginable vehicle. The next morning they lined up on the southern Kansas border. Mr. Melka owned the springwagon and a team of mules. Their position was about eleven or twelve miles west of Caldwell.
...

Father had with him a shovel, a jug of water, (note: no gun) and the flag he was to plant on his claim. Soldiers kept the people out of the Territory until the signal to start, which came at high noon on September 16, 1893. Father rode for about fifteen miles and finally jumped from the springwagon due south from the place he started, and five miles west of Medford, to claim a quarter-section of land.

Father appeared young for his age, and had to show his credentials to prove to cowboys and other land seekers that he was over twenty-one and qualified to make The Run. He was twenty-five years old, and had been in America but five years, so didn't know the English language well yet, but could read, write, and speak both the German and Czech language. He wore out several English-Czech dictionaries....

Mother was one of the first settlers' wives to join her husband in the new land. The folks "built" a dugout to live in and two years later my brother Charles was born. I (Vlasta) arrived on the scene five years after the Opening of the Strip, and by that time, the folks were living in a two-room house. I heard my parents tell of many, many early day experiences, but limit myself to writing of but one.

Goose "Down"

Czech people always raised many geese—the meat for food and the feathers for making pillows and featherbeds. Naturally the folks started raising geese as soon as possible. Instead of buying new lumber to build chicken and hog troughs, it was the custom of the day, and much cheaper, to go to the saloon and buy an empty whiskey keg, cut it in half, and have two watering troughs.

Father bought a similar keg, cut it down, and then filled it with water for the geese. There was enough alcohol in the soaked up keg that when the geese drank from it they died. The pioneers didn't wish to eat the meat, but felt they should pick the geese for their feathers. Since the geese were dead, they decided to pick them thoroughly before hauling them to a ravine in the pasture.

That night the family was awakened by loud honking—the cold night had revived the geese and they came back to the yard. The geese had only been drunk instead of dead. It was hard to keep them warm until the feathers grew out again, but because of necessity, the family managed to do so.

Editor's note: The claim and patent on this land, made out "Grover Cleveland, President of the United States to John Skalnik," remains in the Skalnik family. Anna and Alvin Petrik farm this land today near Caldwell, Kansas.

The Slovak from Cleveland

by Melinda Bradnan

Countless times, I have heard my husband, Michael Bradnan, identify himself as the "Slovak from Cleveland." I know he's aware that he isn't the only Slovak from Cleveland, but he says it with such authority that one takes notice. I have grown to understand and appreciate his allegiance to this heritage. It speaks to qualities of endurance and family loyalty, characteristics essential to immigrant survival in the New World.

Ján and Julianna Brádňan, 1930s

Ján (John) and Julianna Brádňan, Mike's grandparents, immigrated from Klenov, Slovakia in the early 1900s. Ján came first, and worked in a scrap metal yard for a $1.25 a week and saved enough money to send for his family in 1903. His wife Julianna and sons, Ján, age five, and three-year-old Andrej (Andrew) entered their new country through Ellis Island in New York Harbor.

After they joined Grandpa Bradnan in Cleveland, Ohio, he opened a neighborhood saloon. Beer sold for a nickel and shots were a dime. There was a free lunch, prepared by Grandma Bradnan everyday, for whoever happened to be there at noontime.

The saloon prospered until prohibition, when Grandpa opted to close the business. Family members still chuckle when comparing Grandpa's integrity to those saloon owners who decided to stay in business, perhaps not so legally, and became millionaires! Grandpa chose to focus his attention on real estate, and he provided very well for his family.

Grandma Bradnan bore ten children, but only four lived to old age. The eldest son John, at age twelve, was killed when he fell under the wheels of a moving train while gathering coal in "The Flats" with his brother. Four children died as infants from causes that probably could have been prevented given today's medical practice. And the family experienced yet another tragic loss when Paul (Uncle Pauley), the youngest, was killed during World War II. A pilot in the Air Force, he was flying a training mission over the Gulf of Mexico. The Air Force reported that the entire squadron of fully-loaded B-17 bombers was banking left, except the bomber on Uncle Pauley's left made the mistake of banking right. The two planes collided and exploded in mid-air. Paul's body was never recovered, and Grandma Bradnan was never able to accept the reality of his death.

The four surviving boys, from eldest to youngest, Andy, Sam, Michael (Mickey), and John nurtured a family loyalty that intertwined their lives and careers. Andy, Sam, and Mickey went into the grocery and meat market business together. Andy later ventured into the wholesale meat business, and John worked in both businesses until he relocated to California.

Mickey and Sam rented business space as well as living quarters in a building owned by Grandpa Bradnan. They moved the grocery store and meat market into the lower level and their families into the two apartments on the second level. In the 1930s, each family drew $12.00 a week, and enjoyed all they could eat!

My mother-in-law, Marion, loves to tell the story of an anniversary celebration held for Grandma and Grandpa Bradnan. As Mickey and Marion were leaving the party, Marion kissed Grandpa, not just Grandma, on the cheek, and he said, "For that you get $500." She ran to the car to tell Mickey of their impending fortune, but Mickey simply answered, "Ah, forget it, the old man's drunk." But sure enough, the next day Grandpa knocked on the door of their apartment and handed Marion $500, with the instructions that Marion buy a new black dress and Mickey a new suit, adding, "He looks like a stuffed sausage in that old one." She got the new dress, and Mickey got a new suit, and they splurged on a factory rebuilt Hoover. The remainder of their windfall they deposited in the bank—the bank failed a few months later!

Every Friday evening, Mickey and Marion would visit Grandma and Grandpa Bradnan, and, at the same time, take orders for groceries to be delivered in the neighborhood on Saturday. In January of 1938, one night before their regular visit, Andy called Mickey, saying that Grandpa was on a rampage so he was going to pick up Grandma and their little brothers, Paul and Johnny.

The next evening, Mickey found the house dark and silent. Concerned, he called the police. In the basement, they found Grandpa; he had taken his own life. His best suit was neatly laid out on the bed upstairs. Later, the family realized that his outbursts were symptoms of severe depression, a state of mind not uncommon then, but not commonly diagnosed in 1938.

His estate enabled Grandma to maintain her comfortable lifestyle in her own home. As with matriarchs of most families, food is synonymous with her memory. Her "Slavish Coffee," a little coffee with lots of milk and sugar, is fondly remembered, as well as the kettle, which was always on the stove simmering family favorites—sauerkraut and *kielbasa, halusky, paprikash,* lettuce soup, or *baup.*

Uncle Sam visited Klenov in the early 60s, where he found the Brádňan name on a monument in the town square listing names of veterans of the World Wars. The village was under strict communist rule, and conditions were dismal. Relatives located were reluctant to give any information, fearful that their homes might have hidden microphones. The atmosphere did not invite another visit. Uncle Andy tried to keep in touch by mail, but became discouraged when replies read, "Dear Andrew, XXXCENSOREDXXX, Love, Brádňan."

Over the years, the Bradnan family has grown by both descendants and enterprise. The family businesses started by Mickey and Sam are still prospering, and we boast many college graduates, professionals, and successful business men and women. So obviously, my husband Mike isn't the only "Slovak from Cleveland," but he is one of the proudest!

Czech Roots

By Mark Vasko-Bigaouette

My great-grandparents Josef Vásko and Rose (Janda) Vásko left Dolni Cermna, East Bohemia, for America in 1891. They first settled outside Sun Prairie, Wisconsin, where Grandfather Joseph was born in 1892, their first child born in America. A desire to be among fellow immigrants from their homeland led them to seek a more "Czech community," which they found in Silver Lake, Minnesota. Here, Rose gave birth to the last of her twelve children and died in 1919.

Great Grandfather Josef yearned for the "Old Country" and his beloved village so much after Rose's death that he returned there in 1920, leaving his younger children to be raised by his eldest, unmarried son, my Grandfather Joseph.

When the youngest of the children reached eighteen, Joseph sought a bride. Not finding a girl sufficiently "Czech" among his acquaintances, in 1928 he went to Czechoslovakia and lived with his father. While there, he met twenty-one-year-old Mary Kubicek, who was selling vegetables on the town square in Letohrad. A few months later in 1929, they were married in the beautiful St. Wenceslaus Church on the square in Letohrad.

They returned to America and farmed just outside New Prague, Minnesota. Grandmother Mary taught herself to speak, read and write English, learning along with their three children. Reluctant to give up her Czechoslovak citizenship, she only did so in order to cast her vote for President John Kennedy in 1960.

My grandfather Joe died in 1975 at the age of eighty three. Sometime later, my mother Marcella and I understood Grandma's longing for her family, which she hadn't seen since leaving Czechoslovakia in 1928. She especially wished for a picture of the grave site where her mother is buried. This prompted my mother, brother Dan, and myself to travel to Czechoslovakia the summer of 1980.

There we met many relatives, visited the church where my

grandparents were married, and other places related to our family history.

It was a wonderful journey, which inspired me to found the CzechoSlovak Genealogical Society International in 1988, and subsequently resulted in my business of conducting Heritage Tours.

Heritage Tours

As director of Heritage Tours, Mark led his first group of tourists into the newly freed Czech and Slovak Federated Republic (then named) in 1992. Along with regularly scheduled tours, Mark arranges tours for travel agencies, and smaller family groups, and offers assistance in locating family ties. For information about trips conducted by Heritage Tours, write or call Heritage Tours, 4219 Thornhill Lane, St. Paul, Minnesota 55127-7822. (Phone: 1-888-427-8687) Web Site: www.launchpoint.com/heritagetour/index.html

CzechoSlovak Genealogical Society International

With a membership of over 4,000 in 1999, the Genealogical Society has become an important resource for people wishing to document heritage or just seeking "kin" to visit during their travels. Founder MarkVasko-Bigaouette has traced his own family history on two different lines back to the 1400s, finding relatives in several different countries. New members receive an information packet with forms and addresses helpful to starting a search. The Society's quarterly publication provides ongoing information and news of interest. How to join? Write: CzechoSlovak Genealogical Society International, PO Box 16225, St. Paul, MN 55116. For much more information on-line, visit the Society's Web Site on-line: www.cgsi.org

Suggestions about where and how to start a search for your Czech or Slovak ancestry are provided here by Mark Vasko-Bigaouette.

Searching for Czech and Slovak Ancestry
How to Start

1. Fill out an ancestor chart as best you can. The blanks will be filled in as you progress. Document where you get your information.
2. Talk to family members, especially the elderly ones. Use a tape recorder (or video camera) if you can. Look at family pictures, especially older ones.
3. Search through family documents, papers, and Bibles for marriage and baptismal records, births, deaths, pictures. Copy and record all information.
4. Take information to any family reunion or family gathering to compare notes.
5. Research your family group through Federal and State census records as far back as possible.
6. Check County, State, and Historical Society records for: marriages, deaths, probate records, land records, county histories, naturalization and citizenship papers, military records, city directories, old newspapers, fraternal organization records.
7. Look into church records for: marriages, baptisms, deaths. Look for printed church histories. Check the cemeteries.
8. Join the CzechoSlovak Genealogical Society International.
9. Join your local County or State Genealogical Society. Attend meetings of this group. Learn from others.
10. When you feel you have sufficient information to follow, you can begin your research in the Czech or Slovak Republics. The governments are helpful in leading and advising. You may also wish to use private researchers; they are more flexible. A good private researcher will work wherever, take photos, and videotape when possible. If selecting a private researcher, make certain they have good references. The CzechSlovak Genealogical Society International maintains a list of people that they consider trustworthy.

Finding Ancestral Sites in The Czech Republic

by Thomas Danek

Thomas Danek and his wife Frankie, from Pittsboro, North Carolina, joined Heritage Tours to search in 1997 for their roots in the Czech Republic. Tom has a Ph.D. in guidance and counseling from the University of North Carolina at Chapel Hill, and is a state administrator, juvenile services. Here is their story—

As we climbed the narrow dirt road leading up the gentle slope—for the first time—I thought about my ancestor walking down the same hill and passing the same linden trees—for the last time—with his family 145 years ago. Mikulaš (Czech for Nicholas) Danék, his wife Marie Jilek Danék, and their seven children, aged twenty-seven to five, used this very road on their way to the New World in the early 1850s. They left the part of Bohemia known as the Czech-Moravian Highlands (a section traversing eastern Bohemia north to south). Their children and the spouses of those who were married emigrated to Caledonia, Wisconsin. Some of the children moved to the Hutchinson area of Minnesota, after the death of Mikulaš and Marie. The site from which they left the Old World was unknown to their American descendants until June 23, 1997.

What brought our little group—now trodding this ancient path to the crest in the rain, past the newly leafed linden trees—together? This journey really began two years earlier with a mild curiosity about our heritage.

Queries to family members and friends yielded bits of family history recorded over the years by Florence Danek of Minneapolis, John Anderson of Blue Earth, Minnesota, and others. This information was entered into a genealogical database, Personal Ancestral File (PAF) available from the Mormon Church's family history library in Salt Lake City, Utah. From these sources, a descendancy chart for Nicholas and Mary was prepared.

Trips to Minneapolis and Hutchinson, Minnesota, in May 1995 and June 1996, breathed life into the written record. Names became real people who lived and died in real places, and whose graves and home sites could be visited. Family lines appeared. *The History of McLeod County*, found in the Glencoe (Minnesota) Museum, provided photographs. Our curiosity turned to fascination.

Florence Danek introduced us to an article in *The Grass Roots of Racine County Wisconsin*, which provided a brief account of the Nicholas Danéks who left the "Stříteži" region of Bohemia. There are several communities named "Střítež" in the Czech Republic today, so identifying the correct one became problematic.

We visited the Czech Genealogical Society International Facility in St. Paul. Here we were able to identify a number of Danéks from Czech Republic phone books. With the help of the Society, a general letter of inquiry about Mikulaš and Marie Danék was written in Czech. This was sent to the Danéks found in the phone books, which resulted in an exchange of correspondence with Josef and Jana Danék who, though not related, wanted to learn more about the U.S. They live in the Czech-Moravian Highlands region in a town called Hrochuv Tynec, located near the city of Chrudim.

In the fall of 1996, we responded to an advertisement for a tour of the Czech Republic with a genealogical emphasis. This "Festival Tour" combined fun and family research. In preparation for the trip, we sent a descendancy chart to the tour's researcher, who identified a Mr. Josef Jilek living in one of the Střítež communities.

When the tour group arrived in Chrudim on Sunday, June 22, 1997, my wife Frankie and I invited Josef and Jana Danék, along with their friend who could serve as translator, to join us for supper. Having brought a few gifts and mementos from the U.S., I threw a North Carolina State baseball cap into a gift bag for the translator, thinking *he* might like it. As it turned out, their friend and translator Hana Kratochvílová is a beautiful woman who dances professionally with a troupe in Prague. She had learned English from her colleagues in the dance group. She graciously accepted my unusual gift.

Josef had arranged for the five of us to travel as needed the following day in order to follow up on genealogical interests.

The next day after lunch and a walk around the square in the charming city of Polička, we continued on north-northwest to visit Mr. and Mrs. Josef Jilek in Střítež. We stopped at #16, the address provided by our researcher. We were late, and after several persons, two languages, and contacts over a period of weeks were involved in our meeting with the Jileks, the mistake of our arrival at 2:30 p.m. instead of 10:00 a.m. was understood.

We filed through the outside entrance, past the tile stove still radiating heat from the morning's baking, and sat at a table where Mr. Jilek had placed some old family documents. They live at the site where my ancestor Marie Jilek once lived, though the original house has been replaced. This was where my great-great-great grandmother grew up in Bohemia! Euphoria!

The Jileks were familiar with the name Mikulaš Danék, and a neighbor, Mrs. Marie Radiměřska joined in our conversation. Mrs. Radiměřska, a kind and energetic woman with beautiful deep-blue eyes and still wearing her apron, led Josef and Jana Danék, Hana, Frankie and me on our trek on this road up the hill.

The light rain showers stopped, and we gazed at rolling, forested hills beyond the green valley. A few steps further brought into sight an old building overlooking that lovely view. A sign on the building indicated #11. There, still standing, was the home place of Mikulaš and Marie Jilek Danék. Now used for storage, that old structure of stone and brick had served as both barn (lower floor) and dwelling (upstairs) for the family. This apparently was a standard arrangement for farm families of their day.

This was the place they had left, and before that, where they had lived, and hoped, and dreamed. It began to rain again, or so it seemed to me, though the skies were now azure with wispy clouds. I walked ahead of the others—pretending to get a better angle for a picture. After the mist in my eyes cleared, we all strolled to a recently built dwelling nearby, where Mrs. Radiměřska's widowed daughter-in-law lives with her three children.

Our brief visit concluded with a look inside old #11. The keystone entrance and thick stone walls lead to the main room with arched ceiling, hayracks, pitch forks, and other implements silently attesting to the endless hard work of farmers over the centuries.

On the way back down the hill, Marie Radiměřska picked a small branch from the linden tree and gave it to Frankie, who pressed the leaves in a book that evening.

We returned, Mikulaš Danék, with the help of family, friends, effective research, genealogical archives, happenstance contacts, and kind acts; we walked up the hill again to the home you left in order to build anew, and we sensed a homecoming. The Old and New Worlds are much closer now in many ways. It is no longer necessary to choose one, forever excluding the other. And for that we are thankful.

Why did the Danéks leave? We do not have a definitive answer. We have learned that in 1848, all vestiges of the former serf/nobility system were done away with in the Austro-Hungarian Empire. They may have left simply because they were free to do so, and because of promised opportunities in the New World.

©1997 *Thomas Danek*

Note: This Střítež community is located north-northwest of Policka, which is south of Litomysl, the home of composer Bedřich Smetana.

The Mikulaš Danék home in Střítež — Photo by Tom Danek

Touring the Czech and Slovak Republics

Prague

"The Eternal City"..."The Golden City"..."City of Seven Hills"...Prague is as endearing as its descriptions, a city that has truly lived through the centuries. "Going from—toward" is the history of this city as well as the destination of those of us who travel there to experience its charms. "The Eternal City" it is. Prague's position as the crossroads of Europe made it greatly influential for trade since before recorded history. This position has also made it coveted for hundreds of years by invading forces seeking to possess its people and resources.

"The Golden City" enjoyed a golden age, especially during the reign of Charles IV. Under his leadership, Prague grew in magnificence and was larger than Paris or London.

"The City of Seven Hills," Prague is also a city of the unexpected. Despite the fact that its position in Central Europe has placed it in the middle of European conflicts, few cities anywhere can present more than 600 years of architecture and history so untouched by natural disaster or war. Prague delights with lovely views, and its skyline is one of the most beautiful in Europe. Great castles and ornate spires rise gracefully above cobblestone streets, historic parks, cultural centers, indoor and outdoor restaurants, pubs, and cafes. We visited during the height of the summer season, and throngs of visitors created some difficulties with public transportation, but taxicabs were available when necessary.

Prague originally developed as four separate, self-governing towns and a walled ghetto. One should see some of all five spectacular and interesting areas: Staré Město (Old Town), Malá Strana (Little Quarter), Nové Město (New Town), and Hradčany (Prague Castle District), and the Jewish Quarter (Josefov).

The medieval hub of the city is Staré Město (Old Town). This, for many, is the heart of Prague. Its central square, Old Town Square, is now also the center of Romanesque Prague. Through here is the road that connected with the ancient east-west trade route. This square is alive with shoppers, shops and booths alike, and delightful restaurants that serve inside and out.

Old Town Hall and its tower is renowned for its Astronomical Clock, dating from 1410, and the tower affords the tourist a superb view across the Old Town Square. From the tower may be viewed a meandering network of medieval streets which show a town that developed rapidly from necessity. We enjoyed the Church of Our Lady before Tyn, which hovers just off the square. This original structure dates from 1135, and its Gothic steeples are a distinctive feature of Old Town.

On the edge of Old Town is the Municipal House, the supreme showcase for the decorative ambitions of Czech Art Nouveau. First opened in 1912, ongoing renovation has restored the building to its original splendor, a monumental ark in which every aspect of contemporary Czech culture could be shown at its best. The much-restored Powder Gate has been there since the eleventh century, when it formed one of the thirteen entrances to Old Town. This tower acquired its name in the seventeenth century when it served as a storage place for gunpowder.

Old Town sites include unforgettable museums and galleries, churches, historic streets and squares, monuments and buildings, theaters and a palace. Along Charles Street, among the many decorated homes on this ancient street is an Art Nouveau depiction of Princess Libuše, who, according to Slav legend, founded the Premyslids, a family that ruled Prague from A.D. 900 until it came under control of the Austrian Hapsburgs in 1526.

Charles Street merges into the spectacular Charles Bridge, the Bridge of Saints, which features thirty sculptural portrayals of saints from some nine countries, spanning some fifteen centuries. This bridge is easily the most popular historical monument, and it links Old Town to Little Quarter, or Malá Strana.

Little Quarter, on the west bank of the River Vltava, is the second town of Prague. It was founded in 1257, with the aim being to unify scattered Romanesque settlements that had grown up in the shadow of Hradčany (Prague Castle). Little Quarter climbs the slopes that lead uphill to the Hradčany Castle complex. The climb is steep and long, so we opted to start at the castle complex and enjoy the historic walk going downhill.

The Little Quarter Town Hall, the Sternberg Palace, Smiricky Palace, and the baroque Kaiserstein Palace are important buildings on the square. Kampa Island is also a point of interest. Kampa, an island formed by a branch of the Vltava known as the Devil's Stream (Čertovka), is delightful and peaceful. It extends under the Charles Bridge, and has a park that is enjoyed by children.

New Town, Nové Město was established and carefully planned in 1348 by Charles IV to create more market space: Hay Market, Cattle Market, and Horse Market (Wenceslas Square). Twice as large as Old Town and adjacent to it, New Town was also created to make room for the city's booming economy and its increasing numbers of craftsmen, from blacksmiths and wheelwrights to brewers. New Town is imposing and heralds the power and influence it held in medieval times. Wenceslas Square, about 750 metres in length and 60 metres wide, is a spectacular boulevard, bustling with shoppers, making it a contemporary marketplace probably much like it was as a horse market at its inception. Here is a spectacular twentieth century statue of St. Wenceslas on horseback. Just behind the statue of St. Wenceslas is the National Museum, with its monumental staircase, that was completed in the 1890 as another symbol of national awakening.

The State Opera is in New Town, as is the National Theater. The idea for building a Czech National Theater was rejected by the country's ruling Austrians following the Thirty Years' War. Czech national pride began to be restored as Austrian rule relaxed, so the Czechs themselves purchased the land and built this theatre in 1881. Only two months after its completion, the theatre burned down. A testimony to Czech resolve to promote their own culture is that it was rebuilt and reopened just two years later. The theatre was meticulously refurbished in the 1980s. We were thrilled to attend the opera *The Barber of Seville* there. The musical excellence of the performance was heightened by an atmosphere of gilded stucco, crystal chandeliers, and red plush seats and curtains.

The history of Prague begins with the Prague Castle and Hradčany. Founded in the ninth century, it is a commanding center high above the Vltava. St.Vitus Cathedral, on its hilltop perch in the castle complex, is the most distinctive landmark in Prague. Within the complex is a palace, three churches, and a monastery, and since 1918 it has been the seat of the president of the Republic. Václav Havel does not live here (but in a villa), still, he comes here to work! All former Czech presidents have resided in the castle complex.

Around 1320, a town called Hradčany was founded around the castle's exterior. Sights to see in the castle environs are the Royal Palace, St. Vitus's Cathedral, and the Golden Lane of picturesque artisans' cottages along the inside wall of the castle. We strolled down this lane before proceeding downhill to the Charles Bridge.

In the middle ages, two Jewish communities, one from the West and the other from the Byzantine Empire, merged and were confined to an enclosed city. The Jews who lived there suffered from oppressive laws. Discrimination was relaxed in 1784 by Joseph II and the Jewish Quarter was named Josefov after him. The slums of this area were razed in the 1890s, but significant and memorable structures were saved. Among these are the Jewish Town Hall, a number of synagogues, and the Old Jewish Cemetery.

The Old Jewish Cemetery was founded in the first half of the fifteenth century, and its oldest tombstone dates back to 1439. It contains some 12 thousand tombstones, but the number buried there is much greater because the cemetery contains about seven burial layers superimposed one upon the other. In the Jewish Museum is an exhibition entitled "Terezin Painters and Children's Drawings." This exhibit includes drawings of imprisoned children, most of whom died at the Terezin concentration camp. A mere ninety-nine children were spared and 15 thousand were killed at Terezin. This is a startling testimony to the Jewish tragedy of World War II.

As Prague continues "Going from—toward," few cities in Europe approach its appeal in terms of sights and historical and cultural experiences. Here Gothic, Baroque, Romanesque, and Art Nouveau complement one another. Prague offers a concentrated history blended with legends unsurpassed in romance and intrigue. Its beauty, as its name, has endured.

The Charles Bridge

For more than four hundred years, the Charles Bridge was Prague's only river crossing. This magnificent feat of medieval engineering survived floods and wars and, until 1950 when it became closed to motor vehicles, the heavy rolling of motor traffic.

For centuries, the energy of the city of Prague has squeezed through this channel, with crowds of people bustling along for business or meandering for entertainment. The Charles Bridge served as a center of business and buzzed with commercial traffic and sociability. In ages past, justice was administered as convicted felons were thrown from or lowered into the Vltava River to serve their watery sentences. Tournaments have been staged there, as have courtly affairs and, occasionally, a battle. Beneath the bridge, shady riverbanks provided a setting for romance, fun and frivolity. It was, and is today, a center for living.

The earliest bridges to connect the Old Town (Staré Město) and the Lesser Quarter (Malá Strana) were wooden. The first stone bridge across the Vltava was built by King Vladislav I and named Judith Bridge in honor of his wife, Judith of Thuringia. Built between 1158 and 1172, the Judith Bridge collapsed under one of the Vltava's frequent floods in 1342.

Charles IV commissioned a young architect, Peter Parler, to engineer the construction of a new stone bridge, however the bridge was not completed until 1399. It was a forty-seven-year project.

For four hundred years it was known as the Prague Bridge, or Stone Bridge. When this was the only bridge transversing the river, there was no need to specify the bridge by name. Other bridges had not been built when Charles IV embarked on his mid-fourteenth-century program of civic improvements. Finally, in 1870, other bridges had been erected and this impressive example of medieval engineering was named for its patron.

The massive towers at each end, like the bridge itself, were designed for defense. With its width of 33 feet, this bridge could accommodate four carriages abreast. Its 1706-foot span rests on sixteen arches. Today the Charles Bridge is the most familiar monument in Prague. It entertains steady streams of sightseers, souvenir seekers and sellers, and would-be statesmen, and is a popular spot to just "hang out."

For a long period of time, the bridge itself, with its majestic proportions and fine stonework, was the real work of art. Apart from a crucifix, there was no sculptural ornamentation until the end of the seventeenth century.

Then, on the 300th anniversary of the death of St. John of Nepomuk in 1693, the idea of Charles Bridge as a perfect setting for a statue of the saint was conceived. Other statues soon followed, with commemorations by religious institutions, faculties, private donors, and important officials. Some statues are a curious combination of saints that do not share a common theme or chronological base.

Over the next some 250 years, the number of the group of individual statues reached thirty, plus the pillar of Roland (Bruncvik in Czech), legendary hero of the *Song of Roland*, which rests on a bridge pier as patron of the bridge.

Nearly all of the sculptures on the Charles Bridge Avenue of Saints are of Bohemian sandstone, and because of deterioration due to atmospheric pollution, they are gradually being replaced by copies. The originals are held at the Lapidarium, the National Museum's repository of historic stone relics from the eleventh to nineteenth centuries. The Lapidarium also preserves the statue of St. Ignatius of Loyola, which, before it was washed away during a flood, stood at the position now occupied by Saints Cyril and Methodius.

Legends of the Bridge

Legends abound regarding the strength and durability of this magnificent Avenue of Saints. Determined that this bridge was to be the world's strongest, builders supposedly used mortar mixed with the strengthening agent of eggs and, in some versions of the story, wine. Because there were not enough eggs in Prague, citizens from outlying regions were ordered to contribute. Villagers from

Velvary were afraid raw eggs would break and thus sent theirs hard-boiled! Villagers from Unhost sent along cheese, curd, and milk to add to the bonding of the mixture! Whatever the bonding mixture, it worked. This bridge still stands after 400 years!

Another story is that in early Prague, bakers who produced substandard cakes and breads were placed in cages and slowly lowered from the bridge into the river, evidently as a reprimand.

A more gruesome story is one of Protestant leaders hanged in Old Town Square in 1621. The heads of ten were mounted on sticks projecting from the Old Town Tower (Old Town end of the Charles Bridge). As if this story were not grisly enough, the heads supposedly were mounted on this tower for ten years.

Astronomical Clock

Crowds gather on the hour in front of the astronomical clock of Old Town Hall in Prague. Astonished onlookers witness Death (a skeleton) striking a bell every hour while turning an hourglass. As he does so, twelve Apostles, nodding to the crowd, march behind two small windows. On the left side is Paul (with sword and book, Thomas (with a lance), Jude (a book), Matthew (an axe), John (a snake), Andrew (a cross), and James (a mallet). A Turk (recalling sixteenth- and seventeenth-century Turkish invasions) nods his head. Other figures represent fifteenth-century Prague's deepest civic worries: Greed, Vanity, Death, and Pagan Invasion. Then a golden cock shakes his wings and crows to finalize the spectacle!

In medieval astronomy, Earth was the center of the universe, therefore the middle of the clock is a complicated sphere measuring time and showing movement of the moon and sun between signs of the Zodiac.

During World War II, the Nazis blew up the back of the hall, where records were kept, and the clock was damaged but not destroyed. It was restored after the war, and in 1997, more restoration was completed, bringing the clock to its finest glory.

Jewish Monuments in Bohemian and Moravian History

Jews, Czechs, and Germans lived peacefully in Bohemia and Moravia for centuries. Jewish settlements grew naturally among Czech and Moravian villages, towns, and cities. The Jewish cemeteries, splendid synagogues, and burgher houses gradually appeared, adding a mysterious dimension to the splendors of Czech and Bohemian architecture. Prague's Jewish community was first moved into a walled ghetto in about the thirteenth century, because people of Bohemia and Moravia, particularly Christians, were unable to accept Jewish diversity. Still, during reigns of Rudolf II and Ferdinand III they were respected for the ghetto intellectual life and prosperity which flourished. Cruel discrimination existed with the banning from public places, but at the same time, Jewish diligence, thrift, and purposefulness resulted in Jewish fortunes that bank-rolled lavish economic and cultural development.

As Prague's Jewish population dropped in the city center, the Jewish Quarter drifted into disrepair. With public health as the reason noted, the quarter was cleared during 1893-1910. Later, the community itself was nearly wiped out by the Nazis, with nearly three-quarters of the city's Jews dying of starvation or being sent to the death camps. Today only a few thousand Jews live in Prague, compared to some 50 thousand who lived there in the 1930s.

Several synagogues, the Jewish Town Hall, and the magnificent and fascinating Old Jewish Cemetery have been preserved in the former Jewish Town of Prague. Religious services are still held in some synagogues, and historical objects, manuscripts, and prints are exhibited. The Old Jewish Cemetery holds more than 20 thousand gravestones, with the oldest dating back to the fifteenth century. Other wondrous Jewish monuments are in Rakovník, Plzeň, Kasejovice, Březnice, Kosova Hora, Heřmanův Městec, Brno, Boskovice, Velké Meziříčí, Třebíč, Mikulov, Břeclav, Holešov, Přerov, Polná, and Terezin.

Český Krumlov
the special rhythm of another world

The special rhythm is that of a living gallery of picturesque and elegant Renaissance and Baroque-era structures housing homes, cafes, pubs, restaurants, galleries, businesses and shops. It exudes a rhythm the traveler wants not only to learn but to absorb. Beautifully situated on the winding upper Vltava River, Český Krumlov is a uniquely-complete medieval townscape, with arch-covered footpaths and lanes of cobblestone winding up and down steep and narrow corridors. This jewel of a town represents another era, and there is a depth and breadth to the Český Krumlov experience that attunes the traveler to its world in a very short time.

The special rhythm of this southern Bohemia district town, about 105 miles south of Prague, is that of a town that has been bustling since medieval times. Český Krumlov was first mentioned in writing in a 1253 document of the Austrian and Styrian Duke Otakar. When the Krumlov barons built their castle, and ruled the area, it was Chrumbenowe. The name was derived from the old German *krumben ouwe*, meaning "a place on a crooked-shaped meadow." Český, meaning Czech, was added when the town was the seat of Vitek of Krumlov, a member of the Vitkovitz family. The Lords of Krumlov died out in 1302, and their estate was inherited by distant relatives, the Rozmberks. Henry from Rozmberk, the first Rozmberk, and his son Peter helped Český Krumlov attain "town" status more than 600 years ago, a feat that was most difficult to attain. "Town" privileges entailed establishment of churches and monasteries. Handicrafts and trade were encouraged. Then, the Rozmberks turned Český Krumlov into the cultural and administrative center of their domain.

Český Krumlov is split into two parts: there is the Inner Town and there is Latrán, which houses the castle. Both parts of the town lend themselves to hours of strolling. Few cars are allowed.

The center of the town can be reached from all sides. Most visitors park cars or buses in one of two car parks in Jeleni Gardens on the northwest edge of the town. On a walking tour of Inner Town, one will want to see Okresni Muzeum (Regional Museum). Once a Jesuit seminary, dating from 1650–1652, this three-story museum houses an extensive collection of artifacts. Various exhibits and other cultural events are staged there regularly.

Across the street from the museum is the Hotel Ruze (Rose), which, until 1775, was a Jesuit college. The Jesuits were summoned to Český Krumlov in the 1580s by Vilem of Rozmberk. After the Jesuit Order was dissolved there, the building became a barracks, and in 1888 it was purchased to serve as a community center for the Czech population. In 1889 the site became a hotel, but was closed in the 1960s because of disrepair, and was extensively renovated. The adjoining building, the town theatre, was closed in the 1980s, and its interior was reconstructed as an hotel. There are symbols of both the Rozmberks and Jesuits on the building exteriors. The two buildings show the development of architecture, with Gothic, Renaissance, and Rococo influences.

Aside from the mansion tower and the castle building, the most dominant structure in the town of Český Krumlov is the impressive late Gothic Church of St. Vitus. Its graceful, slender tower is visible from every point in the town. From the tower, there is a spectacular view of both Inner Town and the castle across the river. St. Vitus Church arose on the site of a small early fourteenth-century church, and was consecrated in 1439. The main altar, with pictures of St. Vitus and the Virgin Mary, dates from 1673–1683. A niche on the left side of the chapel contains the hearts of some members of the Schwarzenbergs, one of the town's ruling families. There are tombstones of Vilem of Rozmberk and his third wife, Anna Marie of Baden, on the sides of the chapel entrance.

The Town Hall (Radnice), located on the main square, boasts Gothic arcades and has an exceptionally beautiful Renaissance vault inside. Numerous houses with Renaissance facades line the narrow streets, and historic scenes and emblems are everywhere.

Other points of interest include a municipal brewery, salt storehouse, butchers' stalls, the Iron Maiden Tower, which formed part of the town defenses, and the Southern Bohemian Museum.

The Český Krumlov plague column is also a point of fascination. Such columns form statuary in the squares of innumerable cities, towns, and villages in the Czech Republic. They were erected as thanksgiving by the living who were spared during the Black Death, which devastated Europe in the mid-1300s and came closer to exterminating mankind than has any other evil.

In 1374 the original town had only ninety-six houses. Town privileges were expanded and, in 1494, the Rozmberk brothers granted the so-called "royal right" to Český Krumlov, its suburbs and villages. This designation conferred permission to freely leave property to any person, establishment of places where legal disputes and cases could be heard, and an obligation to keep the streets clean. When the last Rozmberk, Peter Vok, grew old and had no offspring, the Český Krumlov estate was sold in 1601 to Emperor Rudolph II. In 1622 the Eggenberks became the town owners. When they died out, in 1719, the Schwarzenberks took over the estate.

Because Český Krumlov has preserved the character of an ancient medieval site, once it is seen it cannot be forgotten. Its uniqueness caused it to be declared a protected urban reservation in 1963. Český Krumlov's importance as an exceptional historical monument was emphasized again in 1992, when the town was entered in the UNESCO World Heritage List, a register of monuments of world significance, "deserving extraordinary care, attention, and support."

Festival of the Five-Petalled Rose
(Slavnosti Pétilisté Ruže)

A festival held during summer solstice in June dramatically and colorfully celebrates the pageantry and history of Český Krumlov. We enjoyed the 1997 Festival of the Five-Petalled Rose.

The significance of the "five-petalled rose" is that of the rose as a symbol of the Rozmberk dynasty. When Henry from Rozmberk divided his kingdom among his five sons, each built a castle and ruled in the following: Český Krumlov, Treboň, Jindřichuv Hradec, Telč, and Sezimovo Ústí. During the festival, Český Krumlov residents dress in Renaissance costumes and move throughout the streets, entertaining festival-goers. The official Saturday parade dramatizes the history of the town, including the five Rose families and their kingdoms. The parade entourage follows a chronological order from the Gothic period, over Renaissance, Baroque, Rococco, and Empire styles until the Classicism of the later Biedermeier period. The magnificence of noble men and ladies is complemented with church dignitaries, soldiers, townfolk, and ordinary peasants, including beggars. Representatives of trade corporations and students make up the end of the parade. Credited in this pageantry are all those who made possible the development of the city of Český Krumlov. The costumed townspeople on parade are delightfully animated, expressive, and entertaining in their various roles!

Five-Petalled Rose on a building in Jindřichuv Hradec.

The parade represents the families of Vitkovitz (Vitek of Krumlov), Rozmberk, Eggenberk, and Schwarzenberk. (English forms of these names include Vittigo, Rosenberg, Eggenberg, and Schwarzenberg.) Musical entertainment is available throughout the town streets, as are booths featuring Czech arts and crafts such as woodworking, toy and puppet making, blacksmithing, straw products, and glassware. Other festivities include street theatre, mock duels "to the death," live chess (chess games with people dressed and acting as pieces), folk music, and fireworks.

The Festival of the Five-Petalled Rose began in 1968 during Prague Spring. It was banned by Communism because it celebrated feudalism, however, it has become an annual event since 1990.

Our party spent three nights in České Budějovice while touring spots in southern Bohemia. We enjoyed the festival's Saturday events. It was also wonderful shopping for authentic handcrafted arts in street booths as well as for garnet jewelry, linens, pottery, and other beautiful items in established shops in the the town. There are many places to stay in Český Krumlov and all of Southern Bohemia.

Krumlov Castle

Krumlov Castle is second in size only to Prague Castle as the largest preserved feudal residence in the country. The most ancient parts are the Gothic round tower of the original *hradek*, Small Castle, and the *horny hrad*, Upper Castle, dating from the first half of the fourteenth century. This massive and sprawling castle dominates the town, both literally and in historical terms. While looking down at the waters of the Vltava River from the Lazebnicky Bridge, the traveler feels as though time has stopped. During the course of six centuries, some forty buildings, five courtyards and castle parks evolved on a high, long domain that is protected on the south by the Vltava River and on the north by the Chvalsinksky Stream.

The castle of Český Krumlov is first mentioned in documents of 1253, when it belonged to the Vitek family. The Lords of Krumlov, as the powerful Czech Vitkovitz family were known, died out in 1302, and their estate was inherited by distant relatives, the Rozmberks. As Český Krumlov was established by the Rozmberks as the cultural and administrative center of their domain, they extended and altered the castle. It became a resplendent Renaissance complex and was the main residence of the Rozmberks, the most politically powerful and wealthy noble family in Bohemia, for nearly 300 years. After Peter Vok Rozmberk, the last of that family, sold his Krumlov estate and moved to Třeboň in 1602, the subsequent owners became Emperor Rudolph II, the Eggenberks, and finally the Schwarzenberks. These owners enriched the castle with many typical Baroque components. By the second half of the nineteenth century, the castle was no longer the permanent residence of the Krumlov-Hluboka branch of the Schwarzenberks. At the beginning of the twentieth century, parts of the castle and mansion were open to the public and, in 1947, the Schwarzenberk property was taken over by the Czech Republic. From the moat with its entertaining brown bears to the ballroom, "Masquerade Hall," Krumlov Castle is an experience to savor.

Český Krumlov also hosts a two-week International Music Festival in August. This event attracts performers from all over the world, and performances are held in nine spectacular settings.

The Beautiful Homelands

Fields of golden canola are grown for cooking oil.

A field of wild red poppies, a brilliant show of color.

Romantic Prague

This capitol city is one of the most beautiful in Europe.
The skyline includes great castles, and ornate spires
of churches and public buildings.

Opposite page:
Astronomical Clock, A.D. 1410

Joan Liffring-Zug Bourret photographs

Historic Bratislava
St. Michael's Gate in Old Town

Performers at the International Folklore Festival at Strážnice, from the Slovak Republic village of Východná near the Tatra mountains, carry this banner featuring beautiful needlework.

Photos by Joan Liffring-Zug Bourret

International Folklore Festival
Strážnice, Czech Republic

Celebrating Mardi Gras

Performers wear village costumes and use noisemakers at the International Folklore Festival. Wheat weaving, a traditional folk art, is used for the ornamentation on the dancer's costume at right.

Mark Vasko-Bigaouette photographs

Mark Vasko-Bigaouette photograph

Performers come also from Silesia, north of Moravia. The Czech crown lands included most of Silesia for hundreds of years.

The little girl is in a Moravian folk dance costume.

Joan Liffring-Zug Bourret photograph

Festival of the Five Petalled Rose

The rose became the symbol of the Rozmberk dynasty, when the kingdom was divided among five sons with a castle for each in five towns. The castle at Český Krumlov is across the river from these performers.

Joan Liffring-Zug Bourret photographs

Czech Marionettes

Traveling marionette companies, in the 1800s–1920s, toured the countryside with programs featuring Czech tales and legends with puppets such as the ones on stage below.

Joan Liffring-Zug Bourret photos

Souvenir stand above is near the Charles Bridge.

Mark Vasko-Bigaouette photograph

Traditional Crafts

The dough birds on sticks are a type of folk decoration found in Southern Bohemia near České Budějovice. Below: Woodcarvings of Jesus, St. Peter, and bees are by Josef Mach, beekeeper who created a small shrine at his home in Southern Bohemia. The legend is that a small thorn pricked Jesus, and before His blood dropped the ground, the drops turned into bees.

Top: Easter eggs with ribbons, a custom in the countryside.

Center: Bagpipe performer from the *Dykyta* folk group from the lake valley area east of Prague.

Left: Doorway decorated for a bride, a Southern Bohemia custom.

Czech Country Scene

Joan Liffring-Zug Bourret ph

Strážnice

Site of the
International Folklore Festival

The largest International Festival of Folklore in both the Czech and Slovak Republics provides a marvelous way to become sidetracked in the Moravian town of Strážnice the last weekend in June.

Strážnice nestles in fertile land along the River Morava, the waterway from which the Moravians took their name when they first settled in that area in the late eighth century. Geographically, the River Morava forms a natural corridor between east and west. At various points the river forms a border between Moravia and Slovakia, and to the south of the Moravian area of the Czech Republic, between Slovakia and Austria. The geography of Strázňice, then, in the center of the Czech and Slovak Republics and at a mid-point in Central Europe, makes it an ideal site for a "center" to celebrate natural origins and culture.

With the exception of thriving local wine caves and the region's notable, lavish wine industry that survived collectivism, for much of the year, the traveler might find this area a bit drab. For most of the year, this area is one through which one travels in order to reach somewhere more interesting. Not so the last weekend in June! Thousands of guests from thousands of miles around converge on Strážnice for the annual and magnificent International Folk Festival staged over three days and nights in three small stadiums built for this event.

Folk music and dancers from the Czech Republic, Moravian area, Slovak Republic, Poland, Spain, Portugal, Italy, and the United States are just a sampling of participants in the 1997 fifty-second annual festival. The tradition of bagpipes, the richness of children's folklore enacted in theatre and music, violinists, legends, dulcimer and brass bands, folk traditions interpreted by men, women, and children's groups are all part of this festival.

During the 1997 festival, the United States folklore contribution consisted of a Civil War Cotillion, a hoedown, and clogging, magnificently performed by students from Utah's Brigham Young University. Never was the fiddling better than in their rendition of "Orange Blossom Special." It brought down the house. Moving, also, was "May the Circle Be Unbroken," the message of which is also the message of the festival itself.

In the peaceful, lyrical countryside surrounding Strážnice, a 32 thousand-year old doll was discovered. About six inches high and featuring big breasts and a big stomach, the doll is said to represent Mother Earth. The bounty of this Mother Earth representation is established also in the purpose of this festival. The goal of the festival is to safeguard traditional culture and folklore. In other words, the tradition of folk culture creating part of a national culture is worthy of not only admiration and respect, but also of preservation that extends to protection as well. Furthermore, the festival philosophy embraces the attitude that knowledge of folk culture fosters international understanding and cooperation.

Any ethnic or religious group seeking to establish methods of preserving their culture will find rich ideas for perpetuating music, theatre, and dance at this festival. Even in the simplicity of the interpretation of children's games, the richness of tradition is celebrated and given sanctuary.

Hotels are booked for miles around during this event. We stayed in Uherské Hradiště (Hungarian Castle), Moravia, about an hour from Strážnice.

May through October in Strázňice, a fine folk museum and a newly-established outdoor museum, with thatched cottages and display of the regional wine industry, are open to visitors.

Folk Museum, Strážnice
Building foundations are painted blue to ward off evil spirits, a medieval tradition.

Peasant Baroque Architecture
Holašovice

Located just west of South Bohemia's main town, České Budějovice, evidence, including name, layout and size, presumes the picturesque peasant baroque village of Holašovice was founded in the early thirteenth century. The village is steeped in tradition, history, and true country style. There were originally seventeen farmhouses; today there are twenty-two. The traditional layout of each farmhouse includes a spacious entry hall leading to a kitchen, a main living room and another small room. There are large tile stoves and cemented oven tops, which were also used as beds for the farm children. Generous gardens encircled by immense stone walls lie just behind the farmhouses. A pond in the village center is used for a supply of water in case of fire, typical for these villages.

Holašovice originally belonged to the Knight of Nemcice, but King Wenceslas II dispossessed the knight of his village because of a supposed treason. The village then was given to the Monastery of Vyšší Brod. During 1518–1520, all inhabitants except one man, a coachman, and one woman died from smallpox. After that plague, Holašovice was populated with settlers from Bavaria. In 1530 all farmhouses were again inhabited, but this time by Germans.

In 1921 there were 211 inhabitants, 63 of whom were Czechs. During those years, Czech and German languages were both used. Children went half of their school years to Czech school and half to German school, a practice which suggests peace and friendship among neighbors. However, in 1938 Holašovice was proclaimed Sudeten by Hitler, and consequently some 60 percent of its inhabitants left the village.

Folklore suggests that, at the beginning of the nineteenth century, there were a number of marriages of girls from wealthy families who demanded beauty in their homes, thus the architecture of the homes of Holašovice today. The village stands as a reminder of beauty created in spite of the harsh conditions of farm life.

Holašovice is one of the Czech Republic's newest UNESCO World Heritage Sites.

Slovakian Showplaces
Piešťany and Bratislava

Piešťany

Life is never going to be quite the same once your passport is stamped Piešťany, the largest spa town in Slovakia. The mineral springs there have been favored by wealthy German-speaking people for many years. Natural spring waters for therapeutic and restorative purposes are on a spa island, cut off from the town's mainland by the beautiful River Vah, a tributary of the Danube.

A lush wooded area and park for peaceful walks, annexes used for mud-wrapping and electro-treatments for rheumatic illnesses, a sanitarium, and facilities for patients wishing to "take the waters," both externally and internally, are all spa attractions. Visitors, in general, may enjoy public swimming pools, picturesque walks along the Vah, and the fun of shopping for Slovakian folk arts. My sister and I, along with most members of our touring group, decided to truly enter the "spa spirit" of healthy restorative measures for mind and body. We did not let the fact that we were not spa patients stand in our way! We all made appointments for a full body massage at a location directly across the street from our hotel. As in every other respect regarding travel in a foreign land, NOTHING about it was quite the same as in the old U.S. of A.!

Our massage day concurred with my sister Joyce's birthday, so we heralded that date with the event as well. Now, my sister, being more liberated than many American middle-class ladies, has a full-body massage monthly in Ottumwa, Iowa. I had never before had a *professional* massage, so Joyce sought to explain the *modus operandi* of the full-body massage to alleviate any modesty concerns she perceived. "Now, Patty, when one has a full-body massage, although you do disrobe, you are given a sheet in which to drape yourself entirely," she explained. "When a leg is massaged, that one leg is undraped (unveiled?) and the massage proceeds. That leg is then draped again, the other undraped, and the massage continues," Joyce elaborated. Now, I was in the spirit of the experience already, but her explanations did, indeed, give me assurance that the event would not be threatening!

We arrived for our massage as scheduled. The room was just large enough for two folding chairs, two masseuses, two customers, and two beds, between which was a rod with a sheet as a curtain. (Now, I soon discovered that that was the *only* sheet on the massage scene.) We were instructed, in Slovak, to place our clothes on the two metal, folding chairs. We complied, and as I awaited my drapery, we were each presented with a hand-sized towel. We climbed upon the beds and, may I say, the towel was not long enough to cover two spots at once—much less three!

"Naked as a jaybird," Joyce laughed quietly.

At one point, about five minutes into the thirty-minute massage, Joyce said from the other side of the curtain, "Still a jaybird," which I knew was her way of noting that she still did not have the promised sheeting either, just in case I thought I was the only one at this disadvantage. The full-body massage was wonderful, consisting of marvelous oils and deep handstrokes and light pats, etc., etc.! It was healthfully invigorating. The only disturbance was that we both had to contain laughter, and that was painful. When we were little girls giggling in church, we had a plan to concentrate on sad events so that we would not break into loud laughter; those same sad subjects were conjured forth during the massage session.

At the end of the thirty-minutes, we stood naked at the folding chairs, hurriedly scrambling through our clothes piled there to sort out the correct American money with which to pay our masseuse. She was impatient to expedite our business and proceed to the next customer. The cost was $22. This business took American currency, which is rare in Slovakia. The patrons for the next appointment popped in as we stood there working out the financial transaction!

Again, the Slovakians do not have our mind-set regarding modesty. A body is just a body, whether it is yours or another's. And, remember, "life is never going to be quite the same again after your passport has been stamped." Amusingly enough, the women masseuses instructed the American men in our group to leave their shorts on. Indeed, in some cases men and women of our tour who were not married to one another were massaged at the same time.

Piešťany had lovely shopping, too. Slovakian shopkeepers, however, do not generally accept Czech money, American Express, travelers checks, American dollars (except at our massage business), or other American credit cards. Simply put, "If you plan to shop, exchange currency at one of the available banks. Shopkeepers do not make impulsive buying easy!"

There were beautiful art galleries and an array of shops featuring products of a wide sphere of traditional folk culture: statuette candlesticks, hand-painted pottery, perforated plates, and china statuettes, cornhusk dolls, wooden pipes, tinker (metal) and horn products, cast metal bells, and chiseled wooden products.

Piešťany is a memorable experience in more ways than several!

Bratislava

There is an old saying that goes, "I was born in Austria. I went to school in Hungary. I grew old in Slovakia. I never left Bratislava, for Bratislava is my home." Indeed, all three countries merge in Bratislava, the capital of Slovakia, which for centuries was an Austro-Hungarian city in which the Slovaks were a distinct minority.

Standing on a steep hillside above the colossal modern-day suspension bridge above the flat plain of the Danube River, one may view all three countries. It is an awesome sight, and it is a sight of the new, upwardly mobile Bratislava that is trying to emerge from the deprivation of forty years under Communism.

With a population of nearly a half million, Bratislava is now a new European capital city and is thoroughly Slovakian. Bratislava has two distinct sections. The old quarter is an attractive slice of Hapsburg Baroque, with the culture of wealth and privilege supporting its housing and business. The rest of the city has the bleak and butchered atmosphere of many modern eastern-European cities with utilitarian, high-rise apartments and morose-looking

Old Town Hall, Bratislava

factories. There are no huge crowds of sightseers, as in Prague, but neither is there the teeming and scheming of unrelenting crowds that Prague holds during the height of the tourist season.

A stroll through and shopping in the narrow streets of the old historical center, lunch at a picturesque sidewalk restaurant, a visit to the charming Bratislava Castle, or a tour of the majestic St. Martin's Cathedral are all delightful experiences.

Bratislava is steeped in history. And both sections of Bratislava, the old quarter and the bleakly modern, have historical stories to tell. The city's location on the crossroads of ancient trade routes is one of the reasons for its continuation. Bratislava first appears in history in A.D. 907 under the name Presalauspurch. It became part of the rising Hungarian state in the tenth and eleventh centuries. In 1465, the first university in Slovakia was founded there, and in 1536 Bratislava was declared capital of the Hapsburg part of Hungary. For more than 200 years, eleven sovereigns (with Maria Theresa being the most famous) and eight sovereign wives were crowned in the Gothic St. Martin's Cathedral.

In 1918 Bratislava became part of the newly-established Czecho-Slovakia, but that hyphen was more than a hyphen to the Slovakians. Slovakia wanted to be an equal partner, not a province. Although Slovakians had linguistic autonomy and political rights, they wanted the same political power enjoyed by the Czechs, who had first billing *before* the hyphen. On January 1, 1993, a new country was established, *no* hyphen!, and Bratislava became its capital.

Folk Arts and Lore

Costumes

Čechy

Costumes from this region are characterized by white blouses with white embroidery, which provide a sharp contrast to the colors of the bodice, skirt, apron and headdress. The bodice can be quite elaborate with gold, garnets or pearls on velvet or brocade. Unmarried girls can wear flowers or bands in their hair, while married women wear caps or scarves. The man's costume is a white shirt with white embroidery, a vest with brass buttons and simple wool pants worn with boots.

Moravia

In this region, the blouses show a contrast of black silk embroidery on white, with colors in the apron and skirt. The girls wear a miniature version of the adult costume. At her wedding, a bride wears a white satin apron with a matching cap. The embroidery on this is done with gold and silver thread. The man's costume reflects the same use of colored embroidery on the shirt and pants. The belt is worn looped around the waist several times. A colorful handkerchief and shiny black boots complete the costume.

Slovakia

Colored embroidery appears on the sleeves, collar and matching cap. These costumes are unique in that the skirt and the apron are identical. Silk ribbons add another touch of color; each ribbon is from a distinct region which can be identified by the pattern of the woven flowers in it.

Slovakian Folk Art

Folk art production is important to both the commerce and culture of the Slovak Republic. Historically, "folk production" was characterized by handiwork in making objects for everyday use from raw materials at hand: clay, stone, glass, metal, wood, textile fibers, horn, leather, wool, dough, and paper.

Folk manufacturers were peasants who had extra time on their hands during winter months to produce various tools, clothes, and functional, but decorative, objects for home use. Other folk artists were village specialists who produced items for others to supplement their incomes, which generally were derived from farming.

Folk art was functional as well as artistic, and the value of its production was noted by the educated class during a Slovak national renaissance in the eighteenth and nineteenth centuries, when they were valued as typical expressions of the Slovak nation.

The artistic expressions of shepherds was a part of their practical life. Shepherd arts include exquisite wood-carved pipes, and Slovak folk musical instruments still found predominantly in the central Slovakia region near Zvolen. Other shepherd arts include dairy farm dishes, cups and tumblers, and moulds for cheeses.

Folk architecture, especially observed in homes and churches, is rooted in its closeness to natural raw materials in the environment. In the Carpathian Mountain region the primary building material was local softwoods, while in the lowlands of the Danube, clay was used. In central Slovakia stone houses can be found.

Products from leather include shoes and boots, bags and belts. Metals find abundance in belt buckles, folk jewelry, hatchets, wooden bowls with metal stud decorations, and cast metal bells. The work that was once produced by the poor wandering tinker, today is produced by acknowledged artists. Horn art includes tubes, salt shakers, and decorative horns.

Artists of both the Czech and Slovak lands are famous for wooden toys, which include horses, cradles, dolls, and puppets. Wood is also fashioned into bowls, boxes, candlesticks, plates, and utensils.

Slovakian earthenware production, both pottery and majolica, are famous worldwide—painted plates, pottery with relief decorations, perforated plates, jugs, flasks, vases, and statuettes. If you have an eye for artistic earthenware, there are factories, such as one in Modra, a short drive from both Bratislava and Piešťany, where you will graciously be given a tour.

Wicker, straw, thin strips of wood, cane, and corn leaves are used to create everything from bread baskets to bowls, dolls, and beehives. Decorative Christmas tree ornaments and batik Easter eggs as well as wooden moulds for honey cakes are popular.

Glass paintings are also favorites of collectors of folk art, as are handmade fabric items like woven aprons, blankets, and patterned rugs. Weaving is more popular in Eastern Slovakia, while the art of embroidery is dominant in Western Slovakia. Through the centuries, embroidery has been influenced by styles of the periods, such as Renaissance or Baroque. Particularly in shops in Western Slovakia's Trnava, Bratislava, and Piešťany, embroidery adorns gowns, skirts and blouses, pictures, bedspreads, and tablecloths.

Bobbin lace making is popular throughout Slovakia and is fashioned sedately in pure white as well as in colorful splashes. Blue and white print fabric is significant in the folk culture of Slovakia. Each county and village has its favorite pattern. Those knowledgeable about folk clothing can "read" in the costumes the village or area from which the wearers come.

Marj Nejdl, folk artist, Cedar Rapids, Iowa

Czech Folk Art

Folk art is largely determined by national consciousness. The three distinct regions of Bohemia, Moravia, and Slovakia tried to foster their own identities. Each area had its traditions in folk arts, which were an important part of celebrating special occasions and fulfilling creative impulses. Similar in materials and artistry, Czech folk art, whether embroidery, jewelry, metal work, wood work, glass and ceramics, toy making, basket making and other symbolic concepts, displays its own unique design as demonstrated on the following pages.

Czech Egg Artistry
(Kraslice)

Kraslice is a tradition that has been passed on to generations of Czechs and Slovaks. Decorated eggshells are mentioned as early as the fourteenth century in Bohemian and Moravian literature, but we know that eggs were symbols of life and hope from the earliest days of Christianity. During the Christian observances of Easter and Christmas, especially, eggs are decorated and eaten as signs of spiritual renewal.

Marj Nejdl
Cedar Rapids, Iowa

Marj Nejdl never thought of her talent for decorating eggs as exceptional. This interest resulted from her exposure to a wealth of Czech culture in her childhood, and Marj continued to practice *kraslice*, Czech egg decorating, in adulthood because she wanted to preserve this aspect of her Czech heritage.

Her father was born near Telc, in the Czech Republic, and came to the United States as a young man to become a partner in a meat market specializing in ethnic meats and sausages in what is now Czech Village in Cedar Rapids. Marj's mother, although born in

Cedar Rapids, was raised in Czechoslovakia in the lace-making town of Zamberk.

As a child Marj learned to decorate eggshells, especially for Easter and Christmas decorations, from an uncle who lived next door. She "thought everybody spent hours and hours decorating eggs." She and her uncle perpetrated their own ideas and designs while enjoying one another's company. Marj began egg decorating in earnest after displaying examples of her work during an extended "Festival of Czech Arts" held at the Cedar Rapids Art Center in 1971. After great success and arousal of public interest at that event, she began demonstrating her skill publically and exhibiting her work in area schools, colleges, and festivals. Her techniques include batik, wax resist, pen and ink, scratching, hand painting, and cut-out "lace" eggs fashioned with a small drill. Formal arts education included commercial art school in Chicago, so eggs are not her only medium. She works also with wood, ceramics, glass, and "anything with a good surface for painting."

Marj's exceptional artistry with traditional Czech folk art has brought the world to her doorstep in rural Cedar Rapids. Since her first public demonstration in 1971, her talent has been celebrated worldwide. She was one of 200 folk artists, throughout the United States, nominated for a National Fellowship Award through the National Endowment of Arts, and has been listed with the Iowa Arts Council as a Master Czech Folk Artist, receiving the Cultural Heritage Fellowship Award from that organization in 1992.

She and husband Ed participated in a two week, 150th-birthday celebration for Iowa held at the "Festival of American Folklife" at the Smithsonian Institute in Washington, D.C., in 1996. Selected from some 700 Iowans interviewed for this honor by the Iowa Arts Council, Ed demonstrated strudel and kolache-making, while Marj exhibited her eggs and displayed the techniques of that art.

Marj has always been active in Czech heritage in the Cedar Rapids area as a Sokol gymnast, folk dancer, and folk singer. She taught gymnastics for Sokol for some twenty-five years, and served ten years on the Board of Directors of the Czech Museum & Library, now the National Czech & Slovak Museum & Library. The Nejdl family continues to hail their Czech heritage with gratification.

Other high points of Marj's career include having decorated eggs for the Archduke of Austria; former First Lady Barbara Bush; Czech Republic President Václav Havel; Slovak Republic President Kováč; Rita Klfmova, Czech Ambassador to the United States, and Astronaut Cernan. Two of Marjorie's eggs were displayed at the Smithsonian Institution.

Daniela Sipkova-Mahoney
Portland, Oregon

Born in Prague, Daniela Sipkova-Mahoney studied international business and foreign languages there. Fleeing the Communist regime, she left Czechoslovakia in the 1980s with her mother, only two suitcases and little money. They booked a tour to Austria, Italy and Germany. While working in the Hospitality and Trade Show Industry in Germany in 1982, she met Patrick Mahoney of Portland, Oregon, who was attending an international automotive trade show in Frankfurt. They married in 1983, and now live in Portland, Oregon with their two children.

Longing for the traditions of Eastern Europe, Daniela became involved in the preservation of Czech and Slovak culture. Drawing from the Czech, Slovak, and Ukrainian designs, she turned to egg decorating, and now displays her talent at craft shows, artist education programs, and workshops nationwide. She has been instrumental in the development of and preservation of cultural crafts and is a part of the Portand area professional teaching program, and also works with the Young Audience Program.

She earned a marketing and accounting degree with honors from Portland State University School of Business Administration. Highlights of her artistic career include the grand opening of MGM Studios in Florida, where she was invited to demonstrate the art of egg decorating. In between working as a part-time accountant and presenting workshops, she decorates hundreds of eggs which are sold through catalogs nationwide and locally in Oregon. She has published a book of paper dolls and a coloring book showing traditional Czech, Slovakian, and Moravian costumes.

Bohemian Garnets

The Czech and Slovak lands abound with legends. There are ancient and medieval legends regarding the Bohemian garnet, which is popular on Czech national costumes and a favorite gem in Czech and Slovak heirlooms, as well as in modern jewelry.

A fourteenth-century reference to the Czech garnet described it as a pyrope "glowing like a flame" on the helmet of the Syrian commander Aretas. The ancients and medieval people believed red stones like garnets, rubies, and bloodstones were remedies for all kinds of hemorrhages. These red gems, which experts call "dove-blood red," also were believed to have a calming effect, and that they could dispel anger and discord. Many garnets were crushed into a powder to be used in ointments or elixirs to strengthen the heart or as an antidote against poisonous snake bites. Because of their red color, they were associated with love, but they were also worn by widows as a consolation after losing a husband.

Worn by people of all social strata—the nobility as well as urban and rural populations—with or without their medicinal value, garnets are still popular. At the time of the National Revival, they were worn as a sign of patriotism. Among the less wealthy, the garnet was often replaced by a glass imitation called a "leon" stone.

The Bohemian garnet, from what is now the Czech Republic, is characterized by a deep red color, and is thought to be the most beautiful red garnet in the world. Other garnets come in a variety of colors, from yellow and green to pink, violet, brown, and colorless. The black garnets from the volcanic tuffs near Rome were used in the eighteenth century occasionally for mourning jewelry. A popular technique with garnets historically was to inlay. The jewels were backed with foils or fabrics and were worn in heavy splendor.

Today jewelry featuring the garnet is made by many different companies which try to create more modern designs rather than traditional styles, but the tradition of the Czech garnet has been preserved mainly in Turnov, the seat of the Granát (Garnet) Cooperative.

The garnet is the January birthstone.

Glassware

Czechs and Slovaks have have had a profound effect on glassware. Czech glass decorators were the first to cut glass with a whirling jeweler's wheel, and thus found ways to engrave beautiful pictures in glass. They were the first to use fluoric acid to etch faces, flowers, and figures in glass. Superb creations from Czech glass artists are found in private collections, museums and royal palaces throughout the world.

Glassmaking began in Bohemia more than 800 years ago, primarily in monastery workshops. Neither World War II nor forty years of communism managed to destroy the Czech glass industry.

Glassblown Christmas ornaments from the Czech and Slovak Republics are famous throughout the world. Some are produced using forms over 1,000 years old. Many have symbolic meanings such as:

* Walnut: Traditional "fruit" of the Christmas season in Central Europe.
* Corn: Symbolizes prosperity, fertility.
* Houses, Churches: Symbols of village life.
* Farm animals: Symbols of everyday village life.
* Birds: Symbols of joy and cheerfulness.
* Swan: Symbol of gracefulness.
* Owl: Symbol of wisdom.
* Spider: In order for the spider to see the beauty of the tall Christmas tree, it scurried up the trunk and along the branches leaving a trail of dusty, grey web.
* Clowns, Carousels, and Circus Animals: The circus was a main entertainment in olden days. Because of its joyful nature, circus characters carried over into joyous occasions.
* Mushroom: The mushroom is indigenous to Central Europe.
* Musical instruments: Symbolize the joy that music brings.
* Stars, Moons, and Angels: Symbolize the closest you can get to heaven.

Traditional Celebrations

Sv. Mikuláš (St. Nicholas)

The devil and the angel walked ahead, signaling the approach of Sv. Mikuláš on December 6, the feast day of St. Nicholas. The devil rattled his chains. The angel wrote with a quill pen as Sv. Mikuláš asked children if they had said their prayers, and whether they had been good or bad. Then, on Christmas Eve, according to the legend, good children received nuts, candy, fruit and gifts. The others received old potatoes.

Sv. Mikuláš, who lived in the fourth century A.D., and became one of the most venerated saints, was Bishop of Myra, the capital of Lycia, an ancient province of Asia Minor, now Turkey. He was especially noted for his charity, and, of course, he was the first Santa Claus.

Christmas

Some of the age-old traditions observed, beginning with Sv. Mikuláš Day and Advent, are a part of preparing for Christmas Day. In ancient times, finding a good husband was of paramount importance to girls, and many pre-holiday games revolved around predictions of just whom a girl would marry. On December 4, St. Barbara's Day, a branch of a cherry tree (or other flowering tree) was broken off and placed in a pot of water in the kitchen; the twig usually burst into bloom at Christmas time, making a festive decoration. The bloom was also considered good luck, and if a girl of marrying age tended it to bloom exactly on Christmas Eve, she was supposed to find a good husband within the year. A further foretelling of the gift of a good husband was dropping melted lead into a pan of cold water; the shape the lead took as it cooled was a forecast of the future husband's occupation. If girls drew sticks from a pile of kindling wood, a long stick meant a tall husband, a thick stick meant a stout husband, and so on.

Traditionally many of the Christmas trees were decorated with handmade ornaments, some using walnut shells and pralines wrapped in colored papers with finely cut and curled edges. Another specialty is the use of eggshells decorated to look like strange fish or representations of the angel who accompanied Sv. Mikuláš. There are colored pinwheels resembling snowflakes and twinkling stars suspended by thread. Gilded walnuts and many varieties of bells are hung in clusters on bright ribbons. A small crèche is often placed at the base of the tree. A blessing is thought to be received if the children spend a night sleeping on a bedding of straw and hay placed near the tree. This custom allows them to take part in the poor and humble birth of the Christ Child.

Traditionally there is caroling in the streets and homes and dancing and eating after the fasting period, which ends on Christmas Eve with a special dinner. It is customary at this time for those who have quarreled during the year to forgive each other publicly.

Carolers go from house to house carrying miniature Bethlehem scenes, and are often invited in for a glass of wine and *vánočka*, a sweet roll filled with almonds and raisins. Little boys dressed as the Three Kings sing for treats, also.

For this season, a large carp may be prepared in four different ways. Best cuts are coated with flour, dipped in egg, coated with bread crumbs, and fried. Lesser cuts are baked "a la black" with prunes and served with dumplings. A third preparation is "a la blue" *(na modro)*. This is carp prepared with gelatin as *"rosol"* and served cold. The head and tail of the carp are wrapped in white cloth and boiled for a soup, usually with finely cut carrots and other vegetables.

Christmas Eve supper might include soup, pearl barley with mushrooms (*Černá Kuba*), carp, fruits and decorated cookies. Carp is the traditional food, but other fish might be served.

Dinner on Christmas day often includes giblet soup with noodles, roast goose with dumplings and sauerkraut, braided coffee cake, kolaches, fruits and nuts, and coffee.

St. Stephen's Day, December 26

The day after Christmas is a day for children to go from house to house caroling, and to receive candies, cookies, and other special seasonal treats.

New Year

Traditionally, it is suggested that one eat pork for good luck and lentils for prosperity on the first day of the new year. If one eats fish, luck would swim away; if one eats poultry, luck would fly away.

Three Kings Day, January 6

In some villages, residents write K † M † B on doorways to bring blessings to the building. Traditionally, three men dressed as the Three Kings would go caroling, and with a piece of chalk blessed by a priest, inscribe Kaspar, Balthazar and Melchior above doorways to bring blessings on that home and family for the year.

St. Joseph's Day, March 19

Czechs think red every year on March 19. St. Joseph's Day is the Czech version of St. Patrick's Day, but there is little religious significance. Instead, it is a day to celebrate the Czech people by honoring the most common Czech name, Joseph. In Czechoslovakia, St. Joseph's Day was always a communal day, an occasion for fun and gaiety. In Cedar Rapids' Czech Village, the taverns serve red beer, the bakeries sell red bread, and the village is decorated with red flowers.

Easter

A custom in both Čechy and Moravia at Easter was that of the boys weaving willow wands and "switching" the girls. This switching was accomplished for many reasons according to the locale. Sometimes girls were switched to get "the devil" or mischief out of them, or so they wouldn't be lazy. Switching also signified the casting off of winter's bleakness and dust. Decorated eggs were given to the tormentors, and virtually everyone, including the family cows and geese, were given eggs for luck in the coming year. When the eggs were eaten, the shells were spread on the fields and garden areas for luck for the growing season.

For Easter, a baked ham or roasted kid (young goat) is featured by many families. The sweet bread (*houska or vánočka*) that is baked for Christmas is the very same dough, round-shaped with raisins and almonds *(mazanec)*, that is almost a must for Easter.

Driving Out Winter, April 30

Spring arrives and the winter witch is burned or drowned. Big bonfires are kindled and a cloth is tied to an old broom to symbolize a witch. The "witch" is burned or thrown into a swift river and drowned. Prague artists make elaborate witches which are taken to an island and burned. Boys return home with a green twig or pine branch to signify the living spring.

Worker's Day, May 1

A holiday celebrated by most European nations.

Saints Cyril and Methodius Days, July 5

Czechs and Slovaks celebrate the Monks Cyril and Methodius who brought Christianity to the Slavs.

John Hus Day, July 6

Celebrated in the Czech lands, but not in Slovakia which does not have this Protestant heritage.

Czech Independence Day

On October 28, Czechs celebrate their independence after World War II. Not celebrated in Slovakia.

Harvest Celebrations

There are two harvest celebrations in the Czech Republic at Thanksgiving time. "Posviceni" is the church consecration of the harvest and "Obžinky" is the secular celebration.

Wreaths made of rye, field flowers and ears of corn are placed on the heads of pretty girls. After the ceremony these wreaths are not destroyed but are saved until the next harvest.

A typical Thanksgiving feast includes: roast pig, roast goose, kolaches filled with prunes, sweet yellow cottage cheese or poppy seed filling, beer *(pivo)* and prune liquor *(slivovice)*.

All Saints' Day
In the Czech Republic, All Saints' Day (Dusicky) is celebrated in November. Like our Memorial Day, it is a time for graves of loved ones to be decorated with flowers and lighted candles.

Wild Mushroom Season

From May to October, gathering wild mushrooms from the woods is a popular and practical pastime in Central Europe. Both Czechs and Slovaks consider the many varieties of seasonal mushrooms as delicacies, whether cooked simply with scrambled eggs, or prepared in any number of original and traditional recipes.

Houby (mushroom) Days' winner, George Tichy, with Pat Martin at the Czech Village annual Houby Days Celebration in Cedar Rapids, 1980.

Photograph by Joan Liffring-Zug Bourret

Czech Tradition

There is an old Czech myth about a king and his three daughters in which the king decided to test his daughters to see which one loved him the most. He asked them what they would give him if they could choose from anything in the kingdom—what would be the most precious thing they would give him?

The oldest daughter said she would give him all the gold in the world. The next daughter said she would give him all the silver in the world. The youngest daughter smiled and said she would give him salt.

The king was outraged to think that his daughter loved him so little as to give him only a common kitchen spice. But the king tried to live without salt in his diet and quickly realized that salt was far-more important than all the gold and silver in the world.

It is customary to this day to welcome a visitor in a Czech home with a slice of rye bread sprinkled with salt.

—*Mana Zlatohlavek, Cedar Rapids, Iowa*

Moravian Folk Custom
Ride of the Kings

Processions, which played at "being king," went around on Whitsun tide to visit Czech, Moravian and Silesian villages. This custom now survives in only a few places, notably the Moravian village of Vlcnov. The "King" and his entourage pass through the entire village on horseback, stopping in front of each house. The "crier" passes either a positive or negative judgement on each dwelling's inhabitants. His proclamations are based upon whether the family appears to have observed or broken the established rules of morality. The truth behind the procession is shrouded in the mystery of ancient times, so participants simply succumb to its enchanting spell. For instance, why is the figure of he king dressed in women's clothing, clenching a rose between his teeth so he is unable to speak? Why are the horses veiled and decorated? There are a variety of legendary explanations, but the charm lies in the glimpse of a world that no longer exists.

The Polka

One of the more widely known dances, the polka was at first a popular round dance, later appearing in the ballroom. It was the last link in the long evolution of peasant dances into social dance. Other dances that existed about the same time were Furiants, Skocnas and Sousedskas. The name polka has sometimes thought to have come from the Czech word for Polish girl, or from the Czech word for half-step because of the heel-toe step in the dance, or from the word pole meaning field. The polka was reputedly first seen danced by a young girl at Elbeteinitz in Bohemia on a Sunday afternoon in 1830. The dance was first introduced in Prague in 1837, and in Vienna, St. Petersburg and London in subsequent years. Wherever it appeared, it achieved an extraordinary popularity, a kind of "polka-mania" with clothes, hats and streets named after the dance.

Keeping stride in the parade of folk dancers, 1997 International Folk Festival, Strážnice, The Czech Republic, this West Texan appeared for the Lone Star State.

Czechs and Slovaks in America
a glimpse of
Sites and Events

The 450 plus Sokol and Fraternal organizations in America have kept alive the traditions of the Czech and Slovak people through their support of literature, dance and music. Large groups of Czech and Slovak populations are found in California, the Dakotas, Iowa, Illinois, Minnesota, Nebraska, New York, Ohio, Pennsylvania, Texas and Wisconsin, and especially in the cities of Chicago, Cleveland, Houston, and Omaha.

In the Midwest and in the Southwest, many Czech and Slovak American communities celebrate their heritage annually. In the old country, a goose or pig, kolaches and beer were festival fare, a tradition still followed today.

Masaryktown—A Bit of Slovakia in Florida

Between 1899 and 1910 thousands of Slovaks came to America. Many were employed in arduous work in coal mines, steel mills, and other industries in the North. In the spring of 1924 the editor of the *New Yorksky Dennik*, a daily Slovak newspaper in New York City, began a series of articles about life and work in Florida, where an easier and more appealing lifestyle was proclaimed. It sounded great. In fact, it almost seemed like paradise for those early shareholders of The Hernando Plantation Company. For a down payment of $1000, each shareholder received twenty acres of land. Next, the task was to find suitable land for growing oranges, and land near Brooksville in Pasco County was selected.

Masaryktown was named for Thomas Garrigue Masaryk, the first president of the then Czechoslovakia. It is located in west central Florida, north of Tampa, about twenty-five miles east of the Gulf of Mexico. Streets are named for American presidents, as well

Milan and Violet Cimbora are shown in front of the Masaryk Hotel and Restaurant building. Violet has established a museum in Masaryktown, Florida's Community Center.

as Czechoslovak poets, writers, patriots, and national heroes.

The now Masaryk Hotel was built originally to serve as a rooming house for men building new homes and as a gathering place for social activities. The Komensky Grammar School, named after the Moravian educational reformer, theologian, and first bishop of the Moravian Church, was started. Orange groves were planted, and onions, sweet potatoes, and cucumbers were tried, but farming the land was unsuccessful. Determined and enterprising, these Slovaks ventured into poultry farming and met with great success. Tampa and St. Petersburg were natural markets. So, The Hernando Egg Producers, Inc. became the largest egg cooperative in the Southeast and Masaryktown became the Egg Capital of Florida!

The small producers of eggs are all but gone in Masaryktown, but Slovak spirit still thrives. There is a library with a sizable collection of books in Czech and Slovak, as well as English. Sokol, a gymnastic organization dedicated to "a sound mind in a healthy body" remains an active community force, and American patriotism is always vigorous.

Slovak roots are cherished in two annual events. The first Sunday in March notes the birthday of Thomas Masaryk, and the last Sunday in October celebrates Czechoslovakian Independence Day. Czechoslovak foods and entertainment abound!

Czech Village, Cedar Rapids, Iowa

In the mid-1800s a military road was established in Iowa for purposes of observation and exploration. This road passed between Dubuque on the Mississippi River and Iowa City. This important trail was located in the path of what today is Highway 1, and ended at Iowa City. Travelers heading west, tired of the arduous journey, liked what they saw in Iowa. A great number of them were from Central Europe, and the lush green hills, fresh streams and rivers reminded them of their homes far away. The Czechoslovakians stayed mostly in the Johnson and Linn County areas, where they homesteaded farms or migrated to the Cedar River shores, which provided a source of food, ice, and transportation. Many of these early settlers started their own businesses, resuming Old Country crafts and trades, and located on the southeast side of of the Cedar River in Cedar Rapids. When a bridge was built to connect the two sides of the area, Czech Village was born. Most of the first business and tradesmen in the Cedar Rapids area were of Czech descent, as were the first mayors, doctors, pharmacists, and lawyers.

The National Czech & Slovak Museum & Library is located in the Village, which brings many tourists and visitors.

Woman tends her geese in the neighborhood near Czech Village. Photographed circa 1949-50, by Joan Liffring-Zug Bourret.

Bohemian Chicagoland

Cermak Road, named for a Czech mayor of Chicago, is a famous street of Czech businesses—bakeries, butcher shops, restaurants, banks and financial institutions. It is the "main line" of Czechoslovakia in Chicago, according to writer Norman Blei. Bohemia begins at 5600 West Central Avenue and ends near Harlem Avenue with Pershing Road on the south, Roosevelt Road on the north. Thousands of Czechs live elsewhere in Chicago, Westchester, and LaGrange, but Cicero and Berwyn have been the ethnic heart of Bohemia in Illinois.

In the June 1979 issue of *Chicago Magazine*, Blei writes that "Bakeries represent the best in old ethnic neighborhoods....the bakeries of Bohemia say, 'Bring me your tired, but mostly your hungry. I'll stuff them with houska and kolacky; I'll make them one of us.'" He adds, "The French have their tarts, the Greeks have their baklava, English their scones. The Bohemians? They just may have it all."

The Cermak Road Business Association sponsors a Houby Parade at the annual Cicero-Berwyn Houby Days. Also in the Chicago area, The Czechoslovak Heritage Museum of the CSA is an important cultural landmark in the Oak Brook area.

The Moravian Folklore Circle of the United Moravian Societies in Berwyn sponsors an annual Moravian Day.

Early twentieth-century stereopticon shows children in national costume, Prague, Bohemia. From the collection of Esther Feske

Texans of Czech descent, from West Texas, march at the International Folk Festival, Strázňice, Czech Republic, 1997.

Czechs, Moravians, Slovakians in Texas

Early Czech-Slovak immigrants arrived in Texas before the battle of the Alamo. They fought for Texas independence. They came by ox cart or wagon, without roads or bridges. The first Czech settlement in Texas (1847) was at Cat Springs in Austin County. Their numbers, influence, and vitality grew and invigorated the area. The development of West, Texas just north of Waco, began between 1850-60 when Anglo-Americans settled a small farming community called Bold Springs. An important factor in the town's establishment was construction of the Missouri-Kansas-Texas Railroad in the 1880s. Thomas M. West owned the only safe in the area and shared it with his neighbors. West conducted so much business for the railroad that the town became known as West, and the name West soon replaced the name Bold Springs.

After World War I, the Czechs, Moravians and Slovaks emerged as the dominant economic and cultural force in the area. Today the Czech and Slovak presence in Texas is more than 700,000. The University of Texas offers courses in the Slavic languages.

West, along with a number of other Texas communities, holds an annual festival. Although visitors come from everywhere, many have Czech, Moravian, and Slovak roots deep in Texas soil. A group is establishing a new museum in the city of Houston.

A Reminder for Those Who Love Peace and Freedom

Sixteen miles to the West of Prague is the village of Lidice, site of a World War II massacre. On the night of June 9, 1942, the German SS, falsely believing the village harbored assassins, burned all the houses to the ground, shot all the adult males, and sent innocent women and children to concentration camps, where many died in the gas chambers. After the war, a new village was built next to the ruins of the old, which is now the site of a rose garden and bronze memorial to the village dead and to all the children who perished in the Second World War. The inscription is written in Czech, English and German.

The Czech and Slovak community of Phillips, Wisconsin, opens its annual June festival with a visit to Sokol Park, where there is a Lidice Memorial serving as a testimonial to the value of freedom.

Memorial at Lidice, The Czech Republic

Photo by Gene Kadlec

Among the Resources

The National Czech & Slovak Museum & Library
Cedar Rapids, Iowa

A fitting tribute to a rich heritage kept alive through centuries of hardships and remarkable achievements, the Museum hosts thousands of guests annually from around the world. For information about programs and events write: National Czech & Slovak Museum & Library, 30 16th Avenue SW, Cedar Rapids, Iowa 52404, or call (319) 362-8500, or log on to web site: www.ncsml.org

The Czech Center, New York City

Part of a worldwide group of centers funded by the Czech government, the Czech Center serves as a gateway for information about all things Czech, whether an event, arts exhibit, or any other field of endeavor. The Center's publication, *Ahoy*, provides a wealth of news involving not only the New York metropolitan area, but other parts of the country as well. Information about the Center can be obtained by writing to: Czech Center, 1109 Madison Avenue, New York, New York 10028. Phone (212) 717-5643

CSA Czechoslovak Museum, Oak Brook, Illinois

A modern Czechoslovak museum which houses books, maps, and records of their membership. CSA is the oldest Fraternal Insurance organization in the USA, currently listing approximately 30,000 members. Write: CSA Czechoslovak Museum, 122 West 22nd Street, Oak Brook, IL 60521-1557. Call (630) 472-0500

Czech Cultural and Community Center, Houston, Texas

A very active group in the Houston area, now located in a mall, but working to raise funds to establish a Czech center in the city's museum district. Write: Czech Cultural & Community Center, 2315 Del Norte, Houston, TX 77018-4792

Slavonic Benevolent Order of the State of Texas (SPJST)

The largest Fraternal Insurance organization in Texas maintains a museum. Write: Slavonic Benevolent Order of the State of Texas, PO Box 100, Temple, TX 76503-0100

Texas Czech Heritage and Cultural Center, La Grange, Texas
This is considered the official Texas State Czech Museum (Center). Write: Texas Czech Heritage & Cultural Center, PO Box 6, La Grange, TX 78945-0006

Czech Elder Hostel Program, Crete, Nebraska
Only one in the United States, but other museums are seeking to establish similar programs. Write: Czech Elder Hostel Program, Doane College, Crete, NE 68333

Czechoslovak Museum in SOKOL, South Omaha
Czechoslovak Museum, 2021 U Street, Omaha, NE 68107-3666

Czech Museum of Wilber, Nebraska
Write: Czech Museum, Main Street, Wilber, NE 68465

National Miss Czech / Slovak USA Pageant
Sponsored by Nebraska Czech Inc., held at the Wilber, Nebraska Festival, first weekend in August. Write: National Miss Czech / Slovak USA Pageant, Chairman John Fiala (currently), 6946 Summerset Circle, Box 5, Lincoln, NE 68516

Many areas with large numbers of people of Czech and Slovak heritage maintain local museums and hold annual festivals. Some of these are located in Illinois, Iowa, Kansas, Louisiana, Maryland, Minnesota, New Jersey, New York, North Dakota, Ohio, Oklahoma, Pennsylvania, South Dakota, Texas, and Wisconsin.

Bohemian National Hall
Cleveland, Ohio

Original drawing by
George Tingwald
for Sokol of Greater Cleveland

Food for Thought
in the words of
Czech Republic President Václav Havel

Excerpted from an address delivered to the National Press Club, Melbourne, Australia, March 29, 1995.

"From different parts of the world, including the Pacific region, we hear voices call the values of Western democracy into question, arguing that they are the creation of a single culture and cannot simply be transferred to other cultures. One typical argument is that Western democracy is marked by a profound crisis of authority, and that without respect for authority as a means of ensuring law and order, society is bound to fall apart.

"But is this crisis of authority a product of democracy? And if so, does it not follow that an authoritarian regime, a dictatorship or a totalitarian system are preferable to democracy after all?

"This is certainly not the case.

"The present crisis of authority is only one of a thousand consequences of the general crisis of spirituality in the world at present. Humankind, having lost its respect for a higher superterrestrial authority, has necessarily lost respect for any earthly authority, too. Consequently, people also lose respect for their fellow humans and eventually even for themselves. This loss of a transcendental perspective, to which everything on this Earth relates, inevitably leads to a collapse of earthly value systems as well.

"Humanity has lost what I once privately described as the absolute horizon, and as a result, everything in life has become relative. All sense of responsibility disintegrates, including responsibility for the human community and its authorities....However, even a decaying or diminishing democratic authority is a thousand times better than the thoroughly artificial authority of a dictator imposed through violence or brainwashing."

Editor's note: *According to legend, the crowned two-tailed lion had been the emblem of the Czech states since the mid-twelfth century.*

*Czech lead crystal vase presented to the
National Czech & Slovak Museum & Library in 1995
by Václav Havel, President of the Czech Republic.*

A Celebration of Traditional Foods Recipes

Illustration by
Bertha M. Horack Shambaugh
(1871—1953), author and artist

Recipes, with minor editing, appear as originally published in The Czech Book: Recipes and Traditions, 1981. *Time and place for many of our friends and contributors have changed, but these morsels of legacy remain. It is our pleasure to carry them on for new generations of readers and cooks.*

Meats and Main Dishes

Marinated Beef
Svíčková

This recipe, one of the great Czech meat delicacies, is by Libbie Urban, a member of Fort Dodge, Iowa's Czech Heritage Board of Directors.

1 large onion
3 stalks celery
1 carrot
1 cup cooked tomatoes
1 Tbs. pickling spice
1 Tbs. mustard
1/4 cup lemon juice
1 1/2 cups water
1 Tbs. salt
6 lbs. beef loin or rump roast
6 slices bacon
4 Tbs. flour
1 pt. sour cream

For brine, boil together all but the last four ingredients. Let cool. Cut fat from the beef and remove bones. Cut bacon slices into 1/2 inch strips. Cut slits in beef and stuff bacon into the slits. Place the beef in a deep dish and pour cool brine (reserve vegetables) over to cover. Marinate in refrigerator two days to one week. The longer the more tender and better flavored. Remove meat from brine. Place in a roaster and arrange vegetables around the beef. Add brine until beef is half covered. Bake at 350° F, covered, until tender.

Pour remainder of brine into a pan and boil for awhile. Remove the beef from roaster when tender and slightly browned. Add the boiled brine to brine in the roaster. Beat the flour into the sour cream and mix into brine. Place beef in this mixture and return to oven, baking uncovered until the top of the gravy appears crusty. Slice beef into thin slices, pour gravy over meat and serve. Two or 3 Tbs. Worcestershire sauce may be added to gravy if desired. This dish can be prepared a day in advance and reheated.

Czech Rolled Beef
Ptáčky

John Kubasta, President of the Cleveland District Alliance of Czechoslovakian Catholics, Cleveland, Ohio

2 1/2 lbs. round steak, cut 1/2-inch thick
salt and pepper
mustard
1/2 pound bacon
2 1/2 large dill pickles
2 medium onions
2 Tbs. shortening
3 to 4 cups beef broth
2 Tbs. flour
1/2 pint sour cream

Pound beef well to make thin 5" x 5" pieces. Season with salt and pepper. Spread slices with mustard. Place 1 slice bacon, halved, and 1/4 pickle, cut lengthwise, on each slice. Slice and sauté 1 onion till transparent. Place one slice on each beef slice. Roll the beef "sandwich" around the pickle. Secure with toothpick. Dice remaining onion and brown in shortening. Place in roasting pan with meat rolls and several cups of beef broth made from beef bouillon cubes. Cover and roast for 1 1/2 hours in a 350° F oven. Baste every 15 minutes with additional broth. Remove meat rolls. Make gravy by adding flour and sour cream to roaster on stove top. Mix and boil. (Mixture will not curdle.) To serve, pour gravy over the beef rolls. Dumplings are a perfect accompaniment.

Czech Village sign

Easter Loaf
Velikonoční Sekanina

Caroline Hruska Sobolik of Spillville, Iowa, wrote, "At Easter, veal was and is our favorite meat. In the late 1890s and early 1900s most families in Spillville raised a hog, a calf, and a few chickens destined to be used toward making the Easter Loaf. I am 85 years old and live on the property which was purchased by my father, Jan Hruska in 1881 for $300. The purchase was on contract, by a handclasp, pay as you can, no witness. Although the wages were $1 to $1.50 per day, repayment was made within a year."

2 cups cooked cubed veal
1 1/2 cups cooked cubed ham
10 eggs, well beaten
1/4 tsp. pepper
1 tsp. salt
1 Tbs. chopped chives or onions
1 clove garlic, chopped (optional)

Combine all ingredients and stir thoroughly. Pour into greased 8" x 8" pan. Bake 45 minutes to 1 hour at 300° F. Cut into squares. Serve warm with celery sticks, or cold with mustard for snacking.

Boiled Beef with Dill Pickle Gravy
Hovězí Maso s Koprovou Omáčkou

Rose and Lumir Vondracek own and operate Vondracek's 16th Avenue Meat Market in the Czech Village, Cedar Rapids.

2 lbs. beef tip (or other beef cut), sliced
3 1/2 Tbs. butter
5 Tbs. flour
2 1/2 cups beef broth
3 medium dill pickles, sliced thin
1 tsp. finely chopped dill (optional)
2 1/2 Tbs. white vinegar
salt and pepper to taste

Boil the sliced beef about 2 hours, or until tender. Melt the butter and mix with the flour. Fry to make light golden roux, add to beef broth along with pickles, vinegar, and dill (optional). Cook for about 5 minutes, or until the gravy thickens. Stir constantly to prevent lumping. Season with salt and pepper to taste. Pour the hot gravy over the sliced beef. Serve with bread dumplings. Use the remaining broth to make delicious beef soup.

Veal Ragout with Caraway Seeds
Dušené Telecí na Kmíně

Helen Secl, Cedar Rapids, Iowa

2 lbs. boneless shoulder of veal, cut into 1" cubes
salt
ground black pepper
3 Tbs. butter
1/2 cup finely chopped onion
2 Tbs. flour
1 1/2 Tbs. caraway seed
1 1/2 cups chicken stock
1 cup thinly sliced mushrooms

Sprinkle veal cubes with salt and a few grindings of pepper. In a 10" or 12" skillet, over medium heat, melt butter, add onion and sauté 6 to 8 minutes or until translucent. Stir in the veal cubes and sprinkle with flour and caraway seed. Stir to coat the veal evenly with the mixture. Cover tightly and cook over a low heat for 10 minutes, shaking the pan every now and then to keep the veal from sticking. Stir in the stock, bring to a boil and reduce heat to low. Add the mushrooms, cover and simmer for 1 hour, or until veal is tender. Add more stock by the tablespoon if the veal seems too dry or the gravy too thick. Taste for seasoning and serve. Delicious over buttered noodles.

Pork Roast
Vepřová Pečené

George Radler of John's Cafe was president of the Czech Catholic Union Fraternal Insurance Society, Cleveland, Ohio.

pork tenderloin roast
salt
1 Tbs. caraway seed
1/2 cup water
3 to 4 Tbs. fat or margarine
1 medium onion, cut in half
1 clove garlic, sliced (optional)

Salt the roast and sprinkle with caraway seed. Place fat up in roasting pan. Add water, fat, onion, and garlic. Cover and roast at 350° F, basting frequently. Add water if needed during baking. When almost done, roast uncovered until meat is tender.

Spareribs and Potatoes
Žebírka s Brambory

On Sunday mornings from 7 to 11, "The Sunday Morning Czech Party" on 1600 KCRG, Cedar Rapids, is hosted by Dave Franklin (David Franklin Kralik, Sr.). His father, Frank, came to Cedar Rapids from Czechoslovakia after World War I. Dave's mother is the former Elsie Hradecky. In his early years, the old-country influence was so strong that upon entering kindergarten, he knew more Czech than English. Dave and his wife, Janice, offer this recipe.

3 lbs. spareribs
salt
1 Tbs. pickling spice
1 onion, minced
2 1/2 cups water
4 potatoes, peeled and cut in half

Place meat, salted to taste, in a small roaster. Sprinkle with pickling spice and onion. Add water, cover, and bake at 350° F until tender. About 1/2 hour before meat is done, add potatoes under the meat. If water cooked out, add a little more. Serve with sauerkraut or your favorite vegetable.

Sauerkraut and Spareribs
Žebírka s Kyseím Zelím

Janice and David Kralik, Cedar Rapids, Iowa

1 lb. spareribs
5 cups water
1 small onion, minced
2 cups sauerkraut (#300 size can)
1 to 2 Tbs. flour

Cook spareribs in water with onion and salt until meat is done. Cut meat into either bite-size pieces or serving size pieces. Measure 2 cups of the broth and add sauerkraut to it. Thicken with flour to gravy consistency, then add cut-up meat. This is best when made a day or two ahead and left in the refrigerator so the flavors can blend.

We enjoy this as a side dish with roast turkey, and make a meal with the leftovers and dumplings.

European Style Paprikas
Uherský Paprikáš

Ann Kenjar, Wenceslaus Square Czech Restaurant, Czech Village, Cedar Rapids

5 large onions, chopped
4 Tbs. shortening
2 pounds beef or pork, cut in 1" cubes
2 Tbs. paprika
1 tsp. salt
1 tsp. pepper
2 cloves garlic, minced
1/4 cup flour
1 cup tomato juice
4 potatoes, cubed
2 cups water
1 cup red wine
1 bay leaf

In a large skillet, sauté the onions in the shortening until brown. Add meat and lightly brown. Add paprika, salt, pepper, garlic, and flour, stirring to coat evenly, and fry for 5 minutes. Add tomato juice, potatoes, water, wine, and bay leaf. Cover and let simmer until potatoes are done.

Butchering the Hog and Making Sausages

Mrs. Marie Klima, Cuba, Kansas

Days are about gone forever when butchering was done at home. This is a memory I'll treasure always. Neighbors or relatives often helped. We didn't have a big black kettle to heat water outdoors. This had to be done in a wash boiler *(vana)* and heated on the wood range. We children couldn't stand the sight of the hog being stabbed, but Mom was right there with the mixing bowl, salt and wooden mixing spoon *(vareka)* to catch the blood for *jelita*. And blood sausage was our favorite. Cleaning the intestines for sausage casings was another unusual task. Later we bought them from the butcher. In preparation for the butchering, Mother baked several loaves of white bread and cooked the barley. We youngsters did our share, such as turning the grindstone while the butcher knives were being sharpened, carrying water, bringing cobs for the fire, chopping onions, and garlic and complaining about our eyes burning. We had the long-handled sausage stuffer, and it was our job to push the handle, not always correctly, but we tried. Father didn't like to use string for tying so he burned off matches and sharpened them. I believe he called them spelky *(spejle)*, sort of like skewers. By poking in and out, the ends were fastened. Browning the *vdolky* in a skillet is about the only way to do them now. However, I remember Mother making stacks of them right on the lids of our wood range.

Czech Sausage
Jaternice

Mrs. Robert E. (Irma) Vanourny of Swisher, Iowa, speaks fluent Czech. Her mother's recipe is a basic recipe and the spices may be cut in half or omitted. "When I was a little girl at home, my mother used to put the meat in a skillet and fry it instead of putting it into casings. That is what I do as well."

1 hog head
2 additional snouts
2 or 3 pork hearts
3 pork tongues
4 pig ears
3 Tbs. salt
3 loaves stale bread
6 cloves garlic
1 large onion
1 Tbs. marjoram
1 Tbs. black pepper
1 tsp. allspice
1 tsp. ground cloves
1 tsp. ginger

Boil all the meat with the salt until tender. Debone and grind. Soak bread in water, squeeze dry and grind with garlic and onion. Mix all ingredients together thoroughly. Stuff into sausage casings. Strain the meat broth and simmer the *jaternice* in it 20 minutes. Rinse in cold water and hang on rods to cool. To serve, fry slowly until brown.

Blood Sausage
Jelita

Irma Konecny Binko, Cedar Rapids, Iowa

1 cup freshly cooked pork
1 Tbs. lard
salt
1 cup barley
1 chopped onion
1/4 tsp. ground allspice
1/4 tsp. ginger
1/8 tsp. cloves
blood

When killing a pig, geese, or ducks, catch the blood and beat with a little salt so it will not clot. (Must be done immediately, for if it clots, it cannot be used.) Salt and boil a piece of pork from the neck or shoulder and a small piece of lard, until done. Cut into small pieces. Cook barley in the broth. Fry onion in lard until golden brown, add spices, barley, meat, and blood. Push into casings and boil in salted water, or bake at 350° F for about an hour or until blood turns color.

Pork Sausage
Jaternice

Adeline Duda Zuber of South Amana, Iowa, offers this family recipe. "This recipe came down through the family without any accurate measurements. A few years ago I decided to write it in pounds and spoonfuls instead of handfuls and 'enough but not too much.'"

- 1 pork heart
- 1 pork tongue
- 2 pork kidneys, cleaned well
- 4 pork ears
- 1 1/2 lbs. pork liver
- 1 1/2 lbs. pork trimmings or roast
- 2 lbs. pork skins
- 1 loaf dry bread, soaked and squeezed dry
- 2 Tbs. salt
- 1 tsp. black pepper
- 2 tsp. ginger
- 2 tsp. cloves
- 2 tsp. marjoram
- 1/3 bulb of garlic, finely sliced into 1 cup of hot broth

Cover all the meat except the liver with boiling water and cook until tender. Remove from the broth. Cover liver, which has been cut into small pieces, with hot broth and let stand. Remove skin from the tongue. Dice all meat and liver and run through a meat grinder, using a medium blade. Mix well and add the bread and seasonings. Mix well again adding another cup of broth.

Stuff into casings (about 12 feet) and tie off in desired lengths. Prick each one 3 or 4 times with a darning needle. Put in the boiling broth and simmer 10 minutes. Plunge into cold water. Place on a rack to cool. Refrigerate up to 2 weeks or put in the freezer. If preferred, the bulk sausage can be put into containers and kept in the freezer without putting it into casings. Before serving, heat it either in a skillet or the oven until it is piping hot all the way through.

Pork Goulash
Vepřový Gulas

Cherryl Benesh Bartunek, Cedar Rapids, Iowa

- 2 to 3 medium onions
- 1/4 cup lard or shortening
- 1 1/2 pounds fresh pork shoulder, cubed
- 1/2 tsp. caraway seed
- 2 tsp. paprika
- salt to taste
- dash of cayenne pepper
- 2 cups water
- 2 Tbs. flour

Sauté onion in lard. Add pork, caraway seed, paprika, salt and pepper, brown well. Add 1/2 cup water and simmer in a covered pan until tender (approximately 1 hour.) Sift the flour lightly over the meat juices and stir until brown. Add the remaining 1 1/2 cups water and simmer 10-20 minutes. Serves 4. Delicious with rice or dumplings.

Wenceslaus Square Goulash
Guláš

Anna Kenjar owns and operates the Wenceslaus Square Czech Restaurant, named after a meeting place in Prague.

- 1/2 cups lard or shortening
- 1 cup chopped celery
- 2 large onions, chopped
- 2 pounds lean pork, cut into cubes
- 2 bay leaves
- 2 cups tomato juice
- 1 Tbs. caraway seed
- 1 cup red wine
- 1 tsp. salt
- 1 Tbs. paprika
- 2 cups water

In a large skillet melt lard, then sauté onion and celery. Add meat and fry until lightly browned on all sides. Add bay leaves, tomato juice, caraway seed, wine, salt and paprika, stirring to coat evenly. Add water, cover and simmer without stirring for 30 minutes. Serve over dumplings. 6 servings.

Pickled Pork Loaf
Huspenina

Mrs. Clarence (Helen Noll) Vlasak's ancestors came to the Dakota territory in 1869. Some of the first settlers in the area, they homesteaded on a farm, which is still in the family, a half mile south of Tabor, South Dakota. "We keep up the family traditions, one of which is making of 'Sulk,' whenever hogs are butchered. Jaternice and koláčes are also traditional foods.

"I am a member of the Czech Heritage Club and teach beginning classes in the Czech language. Also, I have been very active in the performances of Czech plays here.

"During the past 10 years I have visited Czechoslovakia four times and have made many friends there. They are most pleased to learn that we are keeping up the Czech traditions through activities like the Tabor Czech Days, where the Beseda Dance, under the direction of Mrs. Anna Schuch, has as many as eighty people participating."

2 pounds pork hocks
2 pounds pigs' feet
1 pound lean pork
1 tsp. salt
1 Tbs. pickling spice
3/4 cup vinegar
tongue or heart may be added, if desired

Wash meat well, cover with water. Add salt and pickling spice tied in cheesecloth. Boil all together until done. If liquid boils down too much, add water. Remove meat from liquid when tender and chop up or put through coarse meat grinder. There should be at least 3 cups of liquid. Place the chopped meat in the liquid and bring to a boil. Add the vinegar. Let the *"Sulc"* cool and then pour into a 9" x 9" x 2" pan. Place in refrigerator and let set. Skim off the fat and serve cold, sliced about 1/2 inch thick. Keeps in refrigerator for several weeks but must be covered to keep from drying.

Heart in Sour Cream Gravy
Srdíčka na Kyselo se Smetanovou Omáčkou

Leona Netolicky Kaplan, Solon, Iowa

pork or beef heart, cubed (chicken, squirrel or rabbit may also be used)
1 bay leaf
1/2 tsp. allspice
1/2 tsp. peppercorns
1 tsp. salt
1 can evaporated milk or 2 cups heavy cream
1 Tbs. flour in 1/4 cup milk
2 to 4 Tbs. cider vinegar

Combine heart and spices in pan with water to cover. Cook until tender. Add milk and then thicken liquid to gravy consistency with flour and milk mixture. Add vinegar according to taste. Add more salt if desired. This is good served over potatoes or bread.

Rabbit Meat Loaf
Kraličí Pecen

Mrs. George Tichy of Ely, Iowa, learned this recipe from her mother-in-law, Mrs. Anna Tichy, now deceased. When George and his brothers would come home after a day's hunting, this was a little different way of using rabbit. George is well known as a "Houby Hunter" in the Cedar Rapids area.

1 pound ground rabbit
1/2 pound pork sausage
1/2 pound ground beef
1/2 pound ground ham
2 tsp. salt
1/2 tsp. pepper
1 cup bread crumbs
1/2 cup milk
2 eggs
1 onion, sliced

Mix all ingredients, except onion, and shape into a loaf pan. Top with sliced onion, bake for 1 hour at 350° F.

Rabbit with Prune Gravy
Králičí Pečeně se Švestkovou Omáčkou

Fern Fackler of Cedar Rapids serves "Fruit Gravy," made with bits of raisins and prunes, hot at Christmas Eve dinner and cold on Christmas Day. Because there were very few sweet things, this gravy was a real treat, and it was a tradition followed in the home of Fern's mother and father. Depending on whether the Czech family lived near a river or a wooded area, "Prune Gravy" could be served with carp or rabbit.

1 rabbit
1 large onion, quartered
1 bay leaf
2 whole allspice
2 cloves
1 Tbs. salt
12 prunes
1/4 cup raisins
flour
1/4 cup vinegar

Boil the rabbit with the onion, bay leaf, cloves, allspice, and salt. When tender, cut rabbit in small pieces.

Cook prunes and raisins in enough water to cover them until tender; drain, saving liquid. Pit prunes and cut up fine. Using reserved liquid, add enough flour to make a nice thick gravy. Add prunes, raisins, vinegar, and rabbit, and reheat if necessary. Serve over dumplings.

Pickled Fish
Ryba v Rosolu

Janelle McClain, Cedar Rapids, Iowa

raw fish (trout, pike, carp, etc.) cut into 3/4" pieces
2 onions, sliced
2 cups vinegar (Rhine or Sauterne wine may be used instead)
1 cup water
1 tsp. sugar
1 tsp. salt
1 Tbs. pickling spice
2 bay leaves

Bring fish to boil in salted water, then drain. Add onions, vinegar, water, sugar, salt, pickling spice, and bay leaves. Cook until fish is tender. May be canned or placed in refrigerator for 2 to 3 weeks to marinate. During this time bones will dissolve. May be eaten plain or with a sour cream garnish.

Poultry Dressing
Nádivka

Esther Lippert of Cedar Rapids learned this recipe from her mother. It has always been a family favorite and is now also well liked by her daughter's family.

heart, liver and gizzard from poultry
1 slice of pork or beef liver
1/2 small pork heart
1 large onion, chopped
3 to 4 stalks celery, chopped
3 to 4 whole eggs
1/2 tsp. sage
1/2 tsp. salt
1/2 tsp. pepper
1 pint mushrooms, chopped (optional)
1 loaf stale bread, toasted and crumbled

Cook the heart, liver, gizzard, plus extra liver and heart in enough salted water to cover. When tender, remove from liquid and put through the meat grinder. Add celery, onions, eggs, and seasonings. Pour liquid from meat over the bread and add enough milk to moisten. Mix well. Combine with meat mixture. Mushrooms may be added at this point. Add more sage or other seasonings if desired.

If stuffing a fowl, fill loosely as dressing expands when baking. About an hour and a half before fowl is done, pour rest of dressing around the fowl and finish baking. Otherwise, pour into a 9" x 13" greased pan and bake in 350° F oven for 1 to 1 1/2 hours or until done in the middle.

Roast Goose or Duck
Po Českém Způsobu

Virgil and Jitka Schaffer and son Bob, own and operate the Czech Cottage in Czech Village, Cedar Rapids. This charming shop carries a wide variety of imported gifts, antiques, and jewelry. Bob served as president of the Czech Fine Arts Foundation from 1979 to 1981, and the Schaffers have been very important to the establishment of the Czech Museum. Jitka travels to Czechoslovakia at least once a year to buy merchandise and to keep in touch with the relatives there.

1 duck or goose
salt
1 or 2 cloves garlic
dressing (optional) 3/4 cup per lb. of bird

Clean, wash, and dry goose or duck. Rub inside cavity and outside of bird with salt and minced garlic or garlic salt. (If using garlic salt, use less of the regular salt.) Stuff lightly with your favorite stuffing, or leave unstuffed. Czech cooks usually leave bird unstuffed and make dressing in another pan. Place on rack in uncovered roaster, breast side up. Do not cover pan. Roast at 325° F for 40 to 45 minutes per pound for duck or 25 to 30 minutes per pound for goose. During roasting, pour off accumulated fat in pan. Test for doneness by moving drumstick. If it separates easily from the body in the joint, the bird is done. If browning too fast, cover loosely with foil so steam can escape. However, a crisp, brown skin is desired. A 4 to 5 pound duck serves 4. An 8 pound goose serves 5 to 6.

Preserving Eggs

Elsie Chadima found directions on preserving eggs in an old book of her father's. "To each pail full of water, add two pints of fresh slaked lime, and one pint of common salt. Mix well. Fill your barrel half full with the fluid, put your eggs down in it anytime after June and they will keep two years if desired."

Roast Duck
Pečená Kachna

Lad's Tavern in Cleveland, Ohio, is owned and operated by Lad and Agnes Haltuch. Lad immigrated around 1940. Agnes, a native-born American of Czech descent, offers this delicious duck recipe.

1 duck
salt
1 or 2 Tbs. caraway seed
1/2 cup water

Wash dressed duck, salt inside and out, rub with caraway seed inside over duck, place in roasting pan, add a little water. Roast at 325° F, turning it occasionally and basting frequently. When done, drain off most of the grease and allow duck to brown at 375°-400° F. While it is roasting, pierce the skin on the back and under the wings, which allows the surplus fat to escape. This make the skin crisp. Cut into serving pieces and serve with dumplings and sauerkraut.

Chicken Paprika
Kuře na Paprice

Sylvia Benesh Courtney, Iowa City, Iowa

1 stewing chicken, about 4 lbs.
1 medium chopped onion
1/4 cup butter
1/2 tsp. paprika
salt to taste
dash cayenne pepper
1 1/2 cups water
1/2 cup sour cream
2 Tbs. flour

Cut chicken into small pieces. Sauté onion in butter; add paprika, salt, cayenne pepper, and chicken. Brown chicken on both sides; then add water. Cover and simmer until chicken is tender, 45 minutes to 1 hour. Remove chicken to serving platter. Mix sour cream and flour, then stir carefully into pan. Simmer gravy 5 minutes; do NOT boil because the sour cream curdles. Pour gravy over chicken. Serves 4 to 5 people.

Czech Village, Cedar Rapids, Iowa

Savoy Cabbage Deluxe
Výborná Kapusta

This recipe was submitted by "Max" Naxera for his mother, the late Mrs. George J. Naxera. A real family favorite, it was also the recipe of his grandmother, Marie Becicka Hajny "Max," George J. Naxera, Jr., has served as a director of both the Czech Heritage Foundation and the Czech Fine Arts Foundation.

2 cups potatoes, sliced medium thick
6 to 8 cups savoy cabbage,
    cut medium fine
3 Tbs. minced onion, divided
1 rounded tsp. salt
1/4 tsp. caraway seed
2 1/2 cups or more of water, only as
    needed to cook vegetables
1/4 cup shortening
2 to 3 rounded Tbs. flour
2 cups cubed salami

Place potatoes in a kettle, add cabbage and 1 Tbs. of the onion. Add salt, caraway and water. Cook until cabbage is tender. Melt shortening in iron skillet, add 2 Tbs. onion, sauté until soft. Add flour and mix until slightly browned, add liquid from potatoes and cabbage, cooking until it boils gently. Add salami and heat for 1 or 2 minutes. Add to the potatoes and cabbage, mixing gently. Add more salt and a bit of pepper if desired.

Savoy Cabbage and Beef
Kapusta s Hovězím Masem

Mrs. Julia Pazour came to this country at 23 years of age and has lived in southwest Cedar Rapids for many years. Now 84, she is proud to have two children and one stepchild in business in the Czech Village area.

1 small onion, diced
2 Tbs. oil
2 lbs. beef, cut into serving pieces
1/2 tsp. caraway seed
1 clove garlic
2 potatoes, cubed
1 head of savoy cabbage, chopped
2 Tbs. butter
3 Tbs. flour

In a skillet, sauté onion in oil until transparent, then add beef and brown. Add enough water to cover, along with the caraway seed, garlic, and potatoes, and simmer, covered. When meat is almost done, add cabbage and cook until tender. In a heavy saucepan, make a roux from the butter and flour, cook and stir until brown, then add to beef and cabbage. Stir well and simmer a few more minutes. Serve with dumplings.

Czech Ham, Cabbage, and Noodle Casserole
Zapékane Uzené Maso se Zelím a Nudlemi

Sharon Spina Benesh, Milo, Iowa

3 Tbs. butter
1/2 medium size head cabbage, diced
1 small package noodles
2 1/2 cups ground ham
2 1/2 to 3 cups milk
3 eggs, well beaten
1/2 tsp. salt
pepper to taste

Cook the noodles according to directions until just barely tender. Drain.

In a skillet melt the butter and sauté the cabbage until tender. In a 2 1/2 – 3 quart buttered casserole place a layer of half the noodles, then half the cabbage, and all the ham. Then layer the rest of the cabbage and the noodles on top. Scald the milk and slowly add to the beaten eggs, beating constantly. Add salt and pepper and beat well. Pour over casserole layers and bake at 350° F about 1 hour or until a silver knife inserted in the middle comes out clean.

Baked Ham and Noodles
Šunka Fleky

Mrs. Betty A. Losenicky, Cedar Rapids, Iowa, likes to use leftovers of a cheap ham. The ham may be ground or diced according to preference; they always like it ground.

8 ounces medium noodles
2 cups ground or cooked ham
2 cups milk
3 large eggs
1/4 tsp. ground mace
salt and pepper to taste

Cook noodles in boiling salted water until barely tender (do not overcook). Drain well. Combine noodles, ham, milk beaten with eggs, and seasonings. Pour into greased casserole and bake at 350° F for about 1 hour or until center is set. Serves 6.

Black Barley Dish
Černá Kuba

Mrs. Robert E. (Irma) Vanourny, Swisher, Iowa, speaks fluent Czech which she learned from her parents and grandparents.

Mrs. George Tichy, Ely, Iowa, serves this same recipe, adding 1/4 tsp. caraway seed and 2 cloves garlic. The completed dish is served with sauerkraut. This dish was also submitted by Lenore A. Topinka, Cedar Rapids, who adds 1/2 tsp. caraway seed and 1 tsp. parsley flakes instead of sage and majoram.

Mrs. Lumir Kopecky, Cedar Rapids, relates, "Czech Kuba has always been a traditional Christmas Eve dish in the Kopecky family. This goes back to the days when Catholics were not allowed to eat meat dishes the day before Christmas, so Kuba was always the traditional dish for Christmas Eve. We would have with it: koláče, housky, and bábovka served with coffee. The family recipe was meatless."

1 cup barley grits
2 cups water
1 pound pork sausage
1 large onion, chopped
1 cup diced celery
mushrooms, 2 cups or as many as you like, sliced or chopped
salt, pepper, sage, marjoram, and garlic.

Boil grits until tender and most of the water is absorbed. Brown meat, onion, and celery until tender. Add grits, mushrooms, and seasonings to taste. Place in a medium size flat baking dish and bake at 350° F for 1 hour.

Kasparek, Prague's puppet clown

Soups and Stews

Knuckle Bone Soup
Hovězí polévka z kostí

Vlasta V. Kosek, a grandmother to seven, is well known in the Cedar Rapids Czech community. Her husband, Ernest, a veteran of the Iowa State Legislature for 16 years, now owns Ernest Kosek Enterprises (Investments and Real Estate) in Czech Village. Vlasta's grandmother, Ann Jirusche Tomas, came from Chrudin, an industrial town in Czechoslovakia, in 1862 at the age of 4 years. She raised her family on a 289-acre farm near Oxford, Iowa. "We frequently had this delicious, rather substantial soup for lunch. Grandmother Anna, my mothers mother used to say, 'Beef knuckle bones make the best soup stock.' So off to the grocery store I would go to fill a six-quart pressure cooker with beef knuckles. I used to get them for free for the dog. Now, well, they still make a good beef stock."

beef knuckle bones, enough to fill pressure cooker
1 cup or more of celery
1 large onion, minced
1/2 tsp. salt
1/4 tsp. caraway seed
small head cabbage, shredded
eggs, 1 per serving

Clean the knuckle bones and place in six-quart pressure cooker and add water to about 1/4 full. Add the celery, onion, salt, and caraway seed. Pressure cook at 15 pounds pressure for about an hour. Cool until the fat is solidified so it can be removed. Reheat stock to which shredded cabbage has been added. Simmer for 10 minutes, or until cabbage is tender. Poach an egg for each portion on the surface of the liquid.

"With rye bread and butter we needed very little dessert."

Heart Soup
Polévka ze Srdíček

Irma Mouchka Kelly is a kolache baker for St. Ludmila Parish's annual summer kolache festival in Cedar Rapids. Irma says her mother never measured anything with a measuring cup. "Everything was by guess or by golly! Each time we butchered, this soup was our treat."

1 beef or pork heart, cut into quarters
1 tsp. salt
dash of pepper
1/2 tsp. caraway seed
1 medium onion, chopped
1/2 cup flour

Cover heart with water, add salt, pepper, caraway seed, and onion, and bring to a boil. Simmer for about 1 1/2 hours or until fork comes out easily and heart is tender to touch. Remove heart and dice. Thicken liquid with flour. Add heart and serve at once.

Milk Soup
Mléčna Polévka

Times were bleak for many early Czech settlers, and Mrs. Charles (Martha) Krejci of Cedar Rapids often had this as "supper fare" There were always "cracked eggs" to be beaten, and skimmed milk. Cream was sent to a creamery in exchange for butter or a few dollars. "It was a long time before I knew that hens laid eggs that were not cracked."

2 cups milk
1 egg
3 Tbs. flour
pinch of salt

Heat milk to simmer (do not boil) in a saucepan with a tight fitting lid. In bowl mix egg, flour, and salt until smooth, then drizzle into the simmering milk mixture. Cover and let stand 5 minutes. Serves 2 generously.

Liver Dumpling Soup
Polévka s Játrovými Knedlíky

Janice and David Kralik, Cedar Rapids, Iowa

2 pounds boiling beef
8 cups water
2 carrots, sliced
1 onion, minced
2 stalks celery, chopped
1 bay leaf
1 tsp. garlic powder
salt to taste
1 1/2 pounds beef liver
4 whole saltine crackers (16 squares)
1 1/2 tsp. garlic powder
1 tsp. salt
1 egg

Cook boiling beef, water, carrots, onion, celery, bay leaf, garlic powder (1 tsp.) and salt to make beef broth. Grind liver and crackers. Add garlic powder, salt, and egg, mixing well. Bring beef broth to a boil. Dip a large spoon into the broth a few seconds to get it hot. Then dip up a spoonful of the liver mixture, put spoon back into the broth before turning it over. (The liver dumpling should slide off the spoon in one piece. If not, warm the spoon in the hot broth a little longer.) Repeat this procedure until all the liver mixture has been put into the soup. Simmer for 20 minutes. Best when served the next day.

This is a good recipe for people who do not like liver as it takes on the beefy taste of the broth.

Old Fashioned Bean Soup
Fizulová Polévka Po Staru

Mrs. Emil Votroubek, Cedar Rapids, Iowa

1 ham bone
1 1/2 cups dry northern beans
2 medium potatoes, diced
1 medium onion, diced
3 slices bacon
2 Tbs. flour
salt and pepper to taste

Wash beans and place in a large pan with ham bone, potatoes, and onion. Cover with water and bring to boil. Simmer until beans are well done (almost mushy). Add water as needed to keep beans covered. Dice bacon and fry in a medium size skillet to crisp. Add flour, stirring until lightly browned. Add 2 to 3 cups of cooked bean soup to skillet, stirring while it thickens. Pour into soup pot and mix well, adding salt and pepper to taste. Vinegar or catsup may be added to servings at the table, if desired.

Mushroom and Barley Soup
Houbová Polévka s Kroupama

Ernie Hlas, the 1981 president of Czech Village Association, has been in business since 1959 at Ernie's Avenue Tavern in Cedar Rapids.

2 Tbs. butter or margarine
1/2 lb. fresh mushrooms
1/2 cup diced onion
1/2 cup diced celery
1/2 cup diced carrot
1 Tbs. flour
3 cups chicken or beef broth
1/2 cup pearled medium barley
1 1/2 cups cooked chicken or beef
salt and pepper to taste

In a 3-quart saucepan, melt butter, add mushrooms, onion, celery, carrot. Cook over moderately low heat, stirring often, about 10 minutes. Stir in flour, then the broth. Add barley, cover and simmer until barley is cooked through, about 1 hour. Add cooked diced meat, salt and pepper. For a creamy soup, stir in about 1 cup of milk. Reheat and serve in soup bowls. Serves 4 nicely.

Czech Tradition

All those who possibly can will raise their own chickens and hens for eggs, and rabbits for meat. Some will raise goats for milk. Gardens will furnish vegetables of all kinds. Orchards add fruit of every description. This will relieve the family food budget and give the best and freshest produce on the table.

Good Nutrition Soup
Dobrá a Výživna Polévka

Mary Hudecek of Protivin, Iowa, submits this old country recipe which has been in her family for several generations. Mary, a native born Czechoslovakian, is an expert in the art of Czech stitchery. Her work is often displayed at Czech festivals and she conducts workshops for those interested in learning this art.

3 Tbs. vegetable oil
3 Tbs. flour
1/4 tsp. onion salt
3 eggs, beaten
1/4 tsp. black pepper
2 cups water
1 Tbs. chicken soup base
1/2 tsp. celery flakes

Brown flour and onion salt in oil in a skillet over medium heat, stirring all the time. Add the eggs and pepper, mixing very well. Stir until the eggs are done. Add water, soup base, and celery flakes. Simmer 6-7 minutes. Serves 2.
  Serve with rolls of bread for a lunch that's ready in 20 minutes.

Sauerkraut Soup
Zelná Polévka

Rose Bartunek Polehna, Cedar Rapids, Iowa

2 1/2 pints water
1 cup sauerkraut
1 cup cubed potatoes
1 cup sour cream (1/2 pint)
2 Tbs. butter
3 Tbs. flour
1 egg yolk
salt and pepper to taste

Boil sauerkraut and potatoes in water for 15 minutes. Mix together sour cream, butter, flour, and egg yolk, then slowly add to soup mixture stirring constantly. Heat thoroughly until well blended, season to taste and serve. This is usually eaten with boiled potatoes or homemade rye bread.

Mother Vondracek's Tomato Soup
"Rajská Polévka"
dle matky Vondráčkové

Vlasta V. Kosek of Cedar Rapids said this recipe of her mother's is a favorite of the family. Anna G. Vondracek raised her family first on a farm and then in Cedar Rapids.

16 ounces milk
16 ounces pureed tomatoes
1/2 tsp. baking soda (prevents curdling)
salt and pepper to taste (only if using fresh tomatoes)

Heat milk and 1/4 tsp. baking soda in a small saucepan. In a medium saucepan heat tomatoes and 1/4 tsp. baking soda. When both liquids reach boiling point pour together. Do not boil. Soup is ready to serve. Minute rice can be added to the soup if desired, or cooked vegetables such as carrots, celery, etc. Enjoy this family favorite.

Garlic Soup
Česneková Polévka

Bonnie Benesh Samuels, Morning Sun, Iowa

3 cloves garlic (onion can be used for onion soup)
1/2 tsp. salt
1 1/4 boiling water
3 slices rye bread, toasted and buttered

With the back of a spoon, mash garlic with the salt forming a paste. Pour boiling water over the paste and let stand a few minutes. Pour soup over slices of bread which have been placed in serving bowls.
  Garlic soup is considered a preventative of disease.

Potato Soup with Mushrooms
Bramborová Polévka s Houbama

Mildred Drahovzal of Cedar Rapids told us, "My father, Frank Libal, was a cement contractor by trade, and was a very talented man. He spent about 50 years in Czech Divadla *(plays) as a comic although his favorite hobby was horticulture. I always called him the Czech Luther Burbank since he made everything grow. One of the founders of the Cedar Rapids Gladiolus Society, he pollinated 'glads' and had many beautiful seedlings as a result. In 1956, he was awarded the achievement medal from the* American Home *magazine for his original 'Mildred Ann' gladiolus."*

2 quarts water
4 large potatoes, cubed
1 cup mushrooms (fresh, sliced, or dried)
1/2 stalk celery
1 1/2 tsp. salt
2 Tbs. butter
2 Tbs. flour

Put all ingredients (except butter and flour) into pot. Cook until potatoes are done. Remove celery and discard. Mash the potatoes in the soup liquid. In separate pan, melt the butter and add the flour, stirring until medium brown. Add to soup for thickening. Serves 6 with rye bread and butter.

Potato Soup
Bramborovká

Mrs. Louis Novak of Spillville, Iowa, remembers her grandparents, Thomas and Marie Fisher Dvorak, were some of the earliest settlers of this community. "As young people they helped build our St. Wenceslaus Church. A bust of Grandpa is at the Bily Museum, carved by the famous Bily Brothers."

4 Tbs. flour
3 Tbs. shortening
2 medium potatoes, cubed
2 cloves garlic, diced
1 medium onion, diced
1/4 cup pearl barley
1 quart water
1/2 cup dried mushrooms
salt and pepper to taste

Brown flour and shortening in heavy iron skillet, cool and set aside. Cook potatoes, garlic, onion, and pearl barley until done. Add the washed mushrooms and browned flour. Cook a few minutes longer. Add desired seasonings. Serves 4.

Cream of Potato and Onion Soup
Zadělávaná Polévka z Brambor a Cibulí

Kris Barta Jones, an avid horsewoman, is in business with her family at the Saddle and Leather Shop in Czech Village, Cedar Rapids, Iowa.

1 quart cubed raw potatoes
2 Tbs. butter
3 large onions, thinly sliced
3 Tbs. flour
1 Tbs. salt
pepper to taste
1 stalk celery, finely chopped
1 (13-ounce) can evaporated milk with enough water to make 1 quart
shredded Cheddar cheese

Cook potatoes in a quart of water until well done. Drain, reserving liquid. Mash potatoes well and set aside. Sauté onions in butter until light brown. Sift in flour, stirring constantly until blended. Slowly add the reserved potato water and cook until thick. Mix the potatoes with the evaporated milk and water, then add to the soup. Add seasonings and heat through. Serve with a dash of shredded Cheddar cheese. Serves 4 to 6. The recipe may be cut in half for two generous servings.

Mother's Browned Potato Soup
Maminčina Zasmažena Bramborová Polévka

Marie Wokoun, Cedar Rapids, Iowa

2 medium potatoes, peeled and diced
1 medium onion, cut fine
1 clove garlic, mashed
1/4 tsp. caraway seed
1 tsp. salt
pepper to taste
1/4 cup good meat drippings, beef or pork
2 Tbs. flour
dash allspice

Combine potatoes, onion, garlic, caraway seed, salt and pepper. Cover with water and boil until potatoes are soft, then sieve. Save liquid. Brown flour in skillet or oven until a medium brown, add to drippings with a little water, stirring until smooth. Add potato mixture, liquid, and a dash of allspice. If drippings are not available, use bacon bits and bouillon as part of liquid.

Czech Dill Soup
Cěská Koprová Polévka

Mrs. Dennis Dvorak, Cedar Rapids, worked at Sykora Bakery as a young girl.

4 medium potatoes, peeled and cut into eighths
2 cups water
1 1/2 Tbs. flour
1 1/2 cups sour cream
1 tsp. salt
4 to 6 raw or hardcooked eggs
1/2 cup dill greens, chopped

Cook potatoes in water and salt. Do not drain. Mix flour and sour cream in a small bowl. Reduce heat. Slowly stir cream mixture into potato soup. Add boiled eggs, whole or cut. If using raweggs, break directly into soup. Cook only until set as over cooking causes curdling. Sprinkle dill over each serving.

Mother's Potato Goulash
Matčin Bramborový Guláš

Hedvika Konecny Benesh, Cedar Rapids, Iowa

3 to 4 medium potatoes, peeled and cubed
2 large onions, cubed
1 Tbs. caraway seed
1/2 tsp. salt
1/4 tsp. pepper
3 pieces fried down pork, cut into chunks
2 Tbs. flour
1/4 cup water

Boil potatoes, onion, caraway, salt, and pepper in 1 quart of water. When nearly done add the pork and finish cooking until potatoes are tender. Make thickening using flour and a little cold water (1/8 cup), beat, then add a bit more cold water. Stir quickly into goulash to thicken.

Omelette in Milk
Svítek do Mléka

Mrs. Frank W. Novotny and her husband are active in the Czech Heritage Foundation for which Frank served as president from 1980 to 1981. Mae told us, "This is a favorite breakfast recipe, especially on a cold winter morning after coming in from chores. It is also economical since we had our own eggs and milk. The recipe came from Czechoslovakia, given to us by my mother's cousin's family."

2 eggs, yolks and whites separated
3 Tbs. farina or Cream of Wheat
2 cups milk, heated

Beat egg whites until stiff, add pinch of salt. Cream yolks and add to whites. Slowly add farina or Cream of Wheat to the egg mixture. The batter should be the consistency of pancake dough. Pour onto hot greased skillet, browning on both sides. Cut into 1/2-inch squares, drop into hot milk and serve.

Mushrooms, Cabbage and Potatoes

Morel Mushrooms with Beef Sauce
Houby s Hovězí Štávou

Sheryl Bellon is a young registered pharmacist in Cedar Rapids who grew up in the Czech Village area.

1 pint mushrooms, washed and carefully dried
5 Tbs. butter
1 1/2 tsp. minced onion
1/2 tsp. minced parsley
1/4 tsp. salt
1/8 tsp. nutmeg
2 Tbs. flour
3/4 cup beef broth or bouillon
1 tsp. lemon juice (optional)

Slice mushrooms and sauté in 3 Tbs. butter with onion, parsley, salt and nutmeg for about 5 minutes. In separate bowl blend remaining butter and flour, when smooth add broth. Add this to the mushroom mixture and simmer for another 5 minutes. Add lemon juice if desired. If morels are unavailable, *Kozibrada* (goatsbeard) or any fall or spring mushroom may be substituted.

Hot Mushroom Sandwiches
Chléb s Horkými Houbami

Vera Krasova Miller, Cedar Rapids, went mushroom hunting with her father in Czechoslovakia. College in Boston interrupted this activity, so when Vera moved to Cedar Rapids in 1962, she "had to learn from scratch as mushrooms of Iowa were mostly different varieties."

2 cups chopped fresh mushrooms
2 Tbs. butter, softened
1/2 cup mayonnaise
1/4 cup finely diced ham
salt and pepper
4 thick slices French bread
Cheddar cheese, grated

Combine mushrooms, butter, mayonnaise, ham, salt, and pepper. Spread evenly on the four slices of bread. Sprinkle each with Cheddar cheese. Bake in 400° F oven until cheese is bubbly, about 10 minutes. Serves 4.

Mushrooms with Cheese
Houby se Sýrem

Mrs. Lumir Kopecky is a second generation Czech. Her parents came from Czechoslovakia in 1920, and lived in the Cedar Rapids area, where her father was a well-known sausage maker with meat markets in Fairfax and Norway, Iowa. Rose has made many trips back to Czechoslovakia.

1 pound mushrooms, washed and sliced
2 Tbs. butter
1 tsp. flour
1/2 tsp. salt
1 cup *smetana* (sour cream)
2 Tbs. cheese, grated
a few sprigs of dill or parsley, chopped

Sauté mushrooms lightly in butter, stir in the flour and salt. Remove from heat. Blend in the sour cream and sprinkle with grated cheese. Brown under broiler. Serve sprinkled with chopped dill or parsley.

Pickled Mushrooms
Nakladané Houby

Sidonia Klimesh, Spillville, Iowa, says, "This recipe is a popular item at potluck meals and also makes a very nice gourmet gift."

1 1/2 cups vinegar
1 cup sugar
1/2 cup sliced onion
mushrooms

Cook vinegar, sugar, and onion until the onion is nearly transparent. Add the mushrooms, stirring carefully. Let come to a boil and simmer for 5 minutes. Pack into small sterilized jars, pour on liquid, and seal.

Mushroom Loaf
Houbovy Pecen

Elsie Elias of Cedar Rapids is a sister of Lester Sykora and has been involved in the Sykora Bakery business for more than 50 years.

- 1 16 to 20-ounce loaf day-old bead
- 1/2 to 1 cup milk
- 1 pint mushrooms, canned, fresh or cooked
- 3 eggs, slightly beaten
- 1/2 cup chopped onion
- 1/4 cup butter, melted
- 1/4 tsp. paprika
- salt and pepper to taste

Break bread into 1" cubes; place in a large bowl. Add milk just to moisten. Add remaining ingredients, stirring to mix. If dry add more milk to make a pouring consistency. Bake in a greased 9" x 13" pan at 350° F for about an hour or until set.

Cabbage Rolls
Zelníky

Lester Sykora, Sykora Bakery, Cedar Rapids, Iowa

- 4 heads of cabbage
- 3 Tbs. melted butter or margarine
- 1 tsp. salt
- 1 tsp. ground or whole caraway
- 1/4 tsp. black pepper
- egg wash (1 egg and equal amount of water beaten together)
- 1 recipe of your favorite yeast or baking powder dough

Strip outer leaves from cabbage, wash, and drain dry. Shred thinly; cores may be used if chopped fine. Sprinkle cabbage with melted butter, salt, caraway, and pepper. Stir to blend evenly. Put in greased roaster or Dutch oven with lid to keep steam inside. Bake at 350° F for about 1 1/2 hours or until cabbage is tender and tan color. Stir 2 or 3 times so top or bottom will not burn.

Roll dough to about 1/8" thickness and cut into 4" squares. Brush with egg wash or milk. Put tablespoon of filling in center of each square. Bring four corners together and seal seams tightly. Shape into round ball and put seam side down on greased cookie sheet or paper-lined pan. Brush with egg wash. Put in warm draft-free place to rise about 1/2 hour if you use yeast dough. If you use baking powder dough bake at once. Bake at 350° F for 20-25 minutes or until golden brown.

Cabbage can be frozen in an inch-deep pan and cut into 1-inch squares as you use.

Cabbage Cakes
Zelníky

Mrs. Arnold J. (Marie K.) Vileta of Tama, Iowa, offers a bit of old Czech philosophy passed on to her by her mother who died in 1959. "To love the good in people around me, and to avoid the wicked – to enjoy my good fortune and to bear my ill – and to remember to forget – that has been my optimism. It has helped me to live. May it help you too."

- 2 cups finely shredded cabbage
- 2 Tbs. butter
- 1 Tbs. sugar
- 1/8 tsp. pepper
- 1 cake yeast
- 1 1/3 cups milk
- 3 eggs
- 1/2 tsp. sugar
- flour

Stew shredded cabbage with butter, sugar, and pepper. Cool. While cabbage is cooking and cooling, mix batter of yeast, milk, eggs, sugar, and enough flour to consistency of pancake batter. Let rise. When batter has risen and cabbage cooled combine them. Drop batter by spoon onto a well greased shallow baking pan. Bake in a hot oven on one side, then other, until thoroughly baked. These may also be baked on a hot griddle.

Noodles and Cabbage
Nudle s Kapustou

Mrs. Josephine Jungman, Cedar Rapids, has been quilting for years in the Asbury Methodist Church. Quilting has always been a popular Czech community activity.

1 head cabbage
1 tsp. salt
noodles made from 3 eggs (see noodle recipes)
1 small onion, chopped fine
1 Tbs. butter
pepper to taste

Grate cabbage fine, adding salt. Let stand for ten minutes then squeeze liquid out. Cook noodles in salted water, drain and rinse in cold water. In large skillet, sauté onion in butter until golden. Add cabbage and pepper and sauté until transparent. Toss with noodles and serve. May be kept warm in the oven.

Konecny's Cabbage Salad
Zelný Salát

Konecny's Restaurant in Cedar Rapids has traditional family style cooking that attracts people from a wide area.

6 cups sliced cabbage
1 cup finely sliced carrot
1/4 cup sugar
1/2 tsp. salt
1/4 tsp. pepper
1/2 cup milk
1 cup mayonnaise
1/2 cup buttermilk
1/2 tsp. celery seed
3 Tbs. minced dry onion
2 or 3 drops Tabasco sauce

Mix together cabbage, carrot, sugar, salt, pepper, and milk. Cover mixture and refrigerate 15 minutes. Combine mayonnaise, buttermilk, celery seed, dry onion, and Tabasco sauce. Pour over cabbage mixture and refrigerate at least 1 hour prior to serving. Makes approximately 2 quarts of salad.

Cabbage with Caraway Seed Butter
Zelí s Kmínovým Máslem

Marianne Smith, of Marion, works at the Saddle and Leather Shop in Cedar Rapids.

1 medium head cabbage
1/2 inch boiling water in saucepan
1/2 tsp. salt
3/4 tsp. whole marjoram leaves
3 Tbs. butter or margarine
1 tsp. whole caraway seed

Shred cabbage. Place in saucepan with 1/2 inch boiling water, salt and marjoram. Cover. Cook quickly until tender, lifting lid 3 or 4 times to allow steam to escape. Drain. Add remaining ingredients. Serve hot. Serves 6.

Czech Sauerkraut
Kyselé Zelí

Joseph Tesar, Cleveland, Ohio, was president of Karlin Hall which was founded in 1936 by Catholic Workmen Lodges (Katolicky Delnik). "Karlin" is a district of Prague and a nickname for Fleet Avenue in Cleveland, a section settled by Czechs from the area of Pisek and Tabor.

2 reg. cans or 2 pkgs. frozen sauerkraut
1 to 2 tsp. caraway seed
1 large onion, chopped fine
 lard
1 Tbs. flour, or more
1 to 2 tsp. sugar (optional)

Drain liquid from kraut (may be washed and drained again if too sharp), add caraway seed to taste and water to cover. Cook 20 to 30 minutes. Sauté onion in a small amount of lard until onion is light brown. Add flour, (sugar if desired) and cook 5 minutes or until slightly thickened. Remove from stove and add to sauerkraut and cook for 5 more minutes.

Variation: *Mary Barta of Cedar Rapids* adds 1/2 cup pork drippings to this recipe for a special flavor.

Homemade Sauerkraut
Nakládané Zelí

Leona Netolicky Kaplan of Solon, Iowa, still makes sauerkraut every year. "It is a fun day. My family comes over and we have a good time preparing for the winter ahead like happy ants. The kraut cutter we use is 50 years old, but the tub is new, being only 20 years old. In 1980 we made sauerkraut out of 280 pounds of cabbage in one day! I grow the caraway seed for the kraut."

40 pounds of cabbage
scant cup of sugar
scant cup of salt
handful of caraway seed

Remove outer leaves from cabbage, halve heads and remove hearts. Shred the cabbage with a kraut cutter over a large tub. Add sugar, salt, and caraway seed. Mix with hands until juicy. Pack loosely into glass jars, adding juice about level with top. Add one or two hearts to each jar. Put lids on jars as tightly as possible. Store in basement or similar area. Set jars on newspaper and cover with same in case juice leaks out while sauerkraut is working. Do not disturb the jars if they leak, sauerkraut will be all right. Allow to work 4 to 5 weeks. Makes about 15 quarts. One rule of thumb is that 10 pounds of cabbage makes 1 gallon of sauerkraut.

Potato Pie
Bramorový Pecen

Sylvia Benesh Courtney, Iowa City, Iowa

3 eggs
3/4 tsp. salt
1/4 tsp. pepper
3/4 cup milk
3 large potatoes, peeled and grated
3 Tbs. flour
1/4 tsp. baking powder
3 Tbs. bacon fat

Beat eggs, salt, and pepper well; add the milk. Add potatoes then stir in flour and baking powder. Heat bacon fat in large skillet (iron is best) and pour into potato mixture. Dot with butter. Bake in preheated 400° F oven for 1 hour or until golden brown. Delicious with roast pork and sauerkraut.

Potato Mush
Škubánky

Irma Konecny Binko, Cedar Rapids, Iowa

2 1/2 pounds potatoes, peeled and quartered
1/2 cup butter, melted
1/2 tsp. salt
1 1/2 cups flour
1/2 cup ground poppy seed
1/2 cup sugar

Cook potatoes, drain and mash. Make wells in potatoes with the handle of a wooden spoon. Fill wells with the flour. Place over very low heat for a few minutes. Remove and let set 20 minutes, covered. Mix into a stiff dough. Dip a tablespoon into the melted butter, scoop out potato mixture and drop onto buttered platter by spoonfuls. Pour remaining butter over all. Sprinkle with poppy seed and sugar. This is also good with sautéed onions instead of the poppy seed.

Caraway Potatoes
Brambory s Kminem

Jessie Stastny creates Czech costumes and clothes for hundreds of Czechs in the Cedar Rapids area. People throughout the United States write to her at the Czech Closet requesting Czech or other costumes.

4 large potatoes, peeled and sliced
1 small onion, diced
2 Tbs. butter
1 Tbs. caraway seed
1 tsp. salt

In a heavy aluminum kettle layer potatoes and onion. Sprinkle top with caraway seed and salt, dot with butter. Pour enough hot water over potatoes to barely cover. Bring to a boil, simmer for 15 minutes. Serves 4.

Noodles and Dumplings

Homemade Noodles
Domácí Nudle

Sharon Spina Benesh, Milo, Iowa

1 1/2 cups flour
2 eggs, well beaten
1 tsp. oil or melted shortening

Put the flour into a small bowl. Make a well in it and into the well pour the well-beaten eggs and oil. Mix this into a stiff dough. Turn out on a floured surface and knead until very stiff. Roll dough out until almost paper thin. On a clean dry cloth allow to dry partially so dough does not stick together when cutting the noodles. Then cut dough in strips about 2 inches wide. Stack these on top of each other and cut into noodles of desired width. Finished noodles can be boiled in broth or salted water and served as desired. If noodles are not to be used immediately, they should be dried so they do not stick together, and then frozen.

Noodles
Nudle

Helen Horak Nemec, Cedar Rapids, Iowa

2 cups flour
3 egg yolks
1 whole egg
1 1/2 tsp. salt
1/4 tsp. baking powder
1/4 tsp. vegetable oil
1/4 to 1/2 cup water

Measure flour into a bowl. Make a well in center and add egg yolks, whole egg, salt, baking powder and oil. Mix well. Add water 1 tablespoon at a time, mixing thoroughly. (Add only enough water to form a ball.) Turn dough into well floured cloth. Knead until smooth and elastic (about 10 minutes). Cover and let rest ten minutes. Divide dough into 4 equal parts. Roll paper thin. Let dry about 20 minutes on tea towels. Then cut into noodles as desired. Dry about 2 hours. Makes about 6 cups (10 ounces).

Drop Noodles for Soup
Nudličky do Polévky

Nancy Barta and her sister Kris Barta Jones are active members of the Czech Village Association. Their father, George Barta, and the family own and operate the Village's Saddle and Leather Shop in Cedar Rapids.

1 egg, beaten
1 cup flour

Mix in bowl with a fork until well blended and dry and crumbly. Drop little by little into boiling soup stock. These noodles take only a few minutes to cook, and are excellent in chicken stock. For a large kettle of soup (8-quart), double flour and egg ingredients.

Liver Dumplings
Játrové Knedlicky

Mrs. Lumir (Rose) Vodracek of Cedar Rapids noted that it is hard to give exact amounts for ingredients because she cooks like her mother did "handful of this or that." Her husband, Lumir, is the third generation of butchers.

1 pound liver, ground (chicken livers are really good in this recipe)
1 cup bread crumbs
1 small onion, grated or diced fine
2 eggs
1 clove garlic, minced
1 Tbs. chopped parsley
pinch of cloves
pinch of marjoram
salt and pepper to taste
soup stock

Mix all ingredients, except soup stock, very well. Drop by tablespoonfuls into boiling soup stock. Cook about 10 minutes.

Farina Puff
Krupicny Svítek

Cherryl Benesh Bartunek, Cedar Rapids, Iowa

2 eggs, separated
pinch of salt
1/2 to 2/3 cup farina or Cream of Wheat
1/2 tsp. nutmeg
1 Tbs. sugar
2 Tbs. lard
1 cup milk, boiling

Beat egg whites, salt, and sugar until stiff. Add egg yolks and slowly pour in farina to make a batter slightly thicker than for pancakes. Heat lard in iron skillet and pour batter into it. Bake in preheated 400° F oven until done. Cut into wedges and pour boiling milk over it and let steam about 5 minutes. Serve with additional milk if desired, or with dill gravy and roast pork.

Bread Dumplings
Housekové Knedlíky

Mrs. Emil Rezac of Tabor, South Dakota, submitted a bread dumpling recipe "as it is the traditional dumpling for the Czechs, as my husband and I noticed on our various visits to Czechoslovakia. We were many times hosted by our distant relations with a noon dinner which started with soup, followed by the main course: meat, sauerkraut, bread dumplings or potatoes. The dumplings are sliced and look more like oval bread slices. At the end of the feast you take the last pieces of dumpling to sop up the remaining bits of sauce and down the rest of your beer."

1 package of yeast
1 tsp. sugar
1/2 cup milk, scalded and cooled
1 cup milk, warm
1 egg
1/2 tsp. salt
3 1/2 cups flour
3 slices white bread, cubed

Mix the first three ingredients, let set for ten minutes. Mix warm milk, egg, salt, yeast mixture and flour. Add bread and knead. Let rise until double, about 2 hours. Knead again. Divide into 3 long rolls. Let rise about 1/2 hour. Drop one at a time into large kettle of boiling water. Boil about 15 minutes. Remove with slotted spoons onto buttered pan, keep warm. To serve, cut each roll into 8 slices using a thread. Serve with sauerkraut, baked pork, duck or goose. Makes 24 slices, enough for 8-10 people. These freeze well; steam before serving.

Never Fail Toast Dumplings
Zarucéne Houskové Knedlíky

Mrs. Stanley Rejcha of Beatrice, Nebraska, offered this recipe from her ancestors in Czechoslovakia.

1 slice bread, toasted and buttered
1 cup flour
1 tsp. baking powder
1/4 cup milk
1 tsp. salt
1 egg

Cut toast into little squares. Mix all ingredients together. Make an oblong loaf and let rise for 1 hour on breadboard under an inverted bowl. Put in boiling water and boil 10 minutes on each side or until done. Makes one dumpling about 8" long. Cut with string or knife just before serving. Bread cubes are often used in Czech style bread dumplings. Using buttered toast is a nice variation.

Swan near the Charles Bridge

Grandmother's Baking Powder Dumplings
Babičiny Práškove Knedlíky

Dorothy and Ray Snitil are well known for their crafts and woodworking. Ray is in business at Slavia Agencies, Inc. in Cedar Rapids. This recipe was given to Dorothy by Mrs. Albert Fisher who had learned it from her grandmother.

1 1/2 cups flour
2 tsp. baking powder
1/2 tsp. salt (heaping)
1 Tbs. butter
1 egg
milk

Sift flour, baking powder, and salt into mixing bowl. Cut in butter as for pie crust. Beat egg in measuring cup and add enough milk to make 2/3 cup. Pour into flour mixture, stirring lightly until all flour is moistened. It may be necessary to add a few more drops of milk. The dough should not be sticky. Turn dough onto lightly floured board and knead about 20 minutes. Cut dough into 4 parts. Knead each about 10 times. Let rise 5 minutes in a warm place. Half fill kettle with water and bring it to a rollicking boil. Drop the dumplings in, cover and boil 14 minutes. Do not lift the cover until dumplings are ready to take out. Cut with a thread.

Cream of Wheat Dumplings
Krupicové Knedlíky

Mrs. Harry J. (Elsie) Chadima, Cedar Rapids, Iowa, is the daughter of Josef Hajek, who for some 30 years was manager of Svornost, *the oldest Czechoslovakian daily newspaper in the United States. Elsie's father was born in Czechoslovakia in 1866 and studied law at the University of Prague. He began his newspaper work in Cedar Rapids in 1897, with a daily section "Bestnik Iowsky," News of Iowa. Elsie and her brothers or sister would often walk to the post office in the evenings to mail their father's columns and news to the Chicago offices of* Svornost.

While still in Czechoslovakia Josef became friends with Thomas Masaryk, who became president of the Republic of Czechoslovakia, and with the composer Antonin Dvorak. Both of these Czech celebrities visited the Hajek family in Cedar Rapids where her father would enjoy walking and philosophizing with them.

2 cups mashed potatoes
1 cup Cream of Wheat
2 eggs
salt

Mash all ingredients together thoroughly. Form into elongated balls. Boil in salted water for 8 to 10 minutes.

Potato Dumplings
Bramborove Knedlíky

Joe Kocab, Sr. is secretary of Cleveland's Karlin Hall, an organization of 5,800 paid members. Joe's hobby is cooking. He is the Assistant Principal of Cleveland's South High, and has been the radio announcer of "Czech Voice of Cleveland" for 13 years.

3 1/2 to 4 pounds potatoes, cooked in skin, peeled and mashed
2 eggs
2 cups flour
1 Tbs. salt

Mix ingredients well until flour is absorbed. If potatoes are very moist possibly more flour will be needed. Remove dough to a floured bread board and roll out. Cut into dumpling size. Makes around 15. In a large kettle bring water and 1/2 teaspoon salt to a boil. Drop pieces into water and boil for 8 minutes.

Variations:

Mrs. Esther Lippert of Cedar Rapids:
If leftover potatoes are used, put them through a ricer. Grated raw potatoes can be used but water must be squeezed out before mixing them in.

Rose Pecina Cincara received this Sulanky *recipe from her mother Mrs. Frances Pecina,* who came to this country from Czechoslovakia in 1909. Their food was simple with many meatless meals, so the potato was prepared in many ways–potato dumplings, pancakes, soup, *sulanky*, even saving the potato water for rye bread. In 1931 Rose's late husband, Jerry Srp, and the Polehna brothers became partners in a meat market which is still in business in Czech Village, Cedar Rapids.

Sulanky is a dessert variation. To make a topping for the cooked dumpling, fry cooked Cream of Wheat in a little grease until golden. Stir in a bit of sugar. Then add enough water to make the topping a spreadable consistency. Spread this over each dumpling and dot with butter or sprinkle with a cinnamon/sugar mixture.

A second variation is to reduce flour and use farina and half and half when making the dumpling dough. Then stuff each dumpling with pork cracklings or fruit.

Potato Dumplings
Zemiakove Halushky

Elsie Malec is active in the Cleveland Czech community. She caters in her community, her cooking is well known, and she is president of Czech Karlin Hall's Ladies Auxiliary. Her husband, Fred Malec, is a drummer in Czech musical circles.

1 head cabbage, about 2 lbs., finely chopped
3 Tbs. shortening
2 small onions, chopped
1 tsp. salt

Have cabbage prepared before halushky is made. Brown onion in shortening. Add cabbage and salt and fry slowly until browned, about 20 minutes. Set aside until ready for use. Keep hot.

2 large potatoes, grated
1 egg
1 tsp. salt
3 cups flour, approximately

Add egg, salt, and flour to potatoes and mix well. Dough should not be thin. More or less flour may be used according to size of potatoes. Put dough on plate. Use knife to cut off small portion at a time into boiling water. Boil about 15 minutes. Keep stirring to prevent scorching. Drain in colander. Rinse once with water. Do not let *halushky* get cold. Place in bowl. Pour cabbage mixture over *halushky*. Serve hot.

Dumplings
Knedlíky

Anna Kenjar, Cedar Rapids, Iowa

2 cups water
1 tsp. salt
1/2 cup grits
3 cups potato flakes
2 Tbs. butter
2 eggs

In a large bowl mix water, salt, grits, potato flakes, butter, and eggs until smooth. Divide into small balls. Drop into boiling water in a large kettle. Cover and let boil for 15 minutes. Remove and serve.

Sign at an outdoor museum, Czech Republic

My Mother's Fruit Dumplings
Matčiny Ovocné Knedlíky

Alma Turechek is Professor Emerita of music at Coe College, Cedar Rapids, Iowa. Alma's father, Charles, was one of the original 16th Avenue merchants in what is now Czech Village.

1 1/2 cups flour
3/4 tsp. salt
2 rounded tsp. baking powder
2 eggs
milk
fruit: blue plums, fresh cherries, fresh peaches

Sift flour and salt with baking powder. Make a "well" in the flour, add unbeaten eggs. Stir well, adding just enough milk to make a stiff dough. Dough should be handled, but too stiff a dough makes the dumplings tough. Turn dough onto floured board, kneading lightly two or three times. Cut into 4 portions, and roll out into 5- to 6-inch rounds, not too thin. Place 1/2 tsp. flour and 1/2 tsp. sugar into center of each round, spreading slightly. Place sliced fruit over flour mixture. Moisten edges of each round with milk or water and bring together to close completely. Handle carefully do not puncture dough. Drop into a big kettle of boiling water one at a time until they float. Boil 15 minutes or till done, turning carefully once. Gently lift dumplings onto a platter. Brush with melted butter. Blue plums should be halved and pitted. Cherries should be well drained. Peaches should be sliced. The flavor can be enhanced by cooking some of the fruit to make a thin syrup to pour over dumplings.

Plum Dumplings
Švestkové Knedlíky

Marie Wokoun, a native of Cedar Rapids, worked many years as a social worker in New York City. She is a member of the Czech Heritage Foundation.

3 Tbs. butter or margarine
2 cups flour
2 cups cooked, mashed, sieved potatoes
1 tsp. salt
2 eggs, slightly beaten
plums, washed and dried

Cut the butter into the flour until fine as cornmeal. Add the mashed potatoes, eggs, and salt, mixing until smooth. Roll out to 1/4 inch thickness and cut into 3- to 4-inch squares. Place a plum on each piece and carefully and completely surround with dough. Gently put a few at a time into boiling water, not allowing the water to boil too vigorously. Cook about 15 minutes. Check often while cooking. These may be steamed instead, if desired. Serve with melted butter, sugar and cinnamon, or even a little cottage cheese. Some people like them with buttered and browned bread crumbs.

Prune Dumplings
Švestkové Knedlíky

Mrs. Wencil (Esther) Lippert of Cedar Rapids says, "my mother made these dumplings when I was a child. I continued making them and when I married, they were a favorite with the whole family. Even our grandson enjoys making them. Also our son, who enjoys cooking, makes them. We have even passed them along to a niece."

2 eggs, slightly beaten
1/2 cup milk
2 to 2 1/2 cups flour, unsifted
1 tsp. salt
24 prunes

Mix all ingredients, except prunes, together. If necessary mix in a little more flour so dough will not be sticky. Take a teaspoon of dough (the size of a walnut) and pat into a circle on a floured board, enough to cover one prune, pinch dough tightly around prune. Cook in boiling salted water about 15 minutes. Cut one in half to see if done, if not, cook 5 minutes longer. Cut and serve with hot melted butter and sprinkle with cinnamon and sugar. Makes about 2 dozen.

Yeast Breads

Bohemian Rye Bread
Žitný Chléb

Mana Zlatohlavek, Cedař Rapids, who came to the United States with her parents when she was 7 years old, says, "In Czechoslovakia we did not have white bread, only rye, so it took us quite a long time to get used to eating white bread."

1 small cake yeast
1 tsp. sugar
1/2 cup lukewarm water
2 cups warm water or potato water
3 cups rye flour
2 Tbs. melted lard
1 Tbs. caraway seed
3 cups additional rye flour
1 cup white flour
1 Tbs. salt

Combine yeast, sugar, and 1/2 cup warm water and set in warm place for 5 minutes. Add 2 cups warm water or potato water, 3 cups rye flour, melted shortening and caraway seed. Mix well with a wooden spoon, cover with waxed paper and let rise in warm place for 2 hours. It will be bubbly on top. Add remaining flour and salt. Mix well, then knead on bread board thoroughly, kneading in more flour if necessary, so it is not sticky. Form into large ball, return to a greased bowl and sprinkle lightly with flour. Cover and let rise about 1 3/4 hours or until light and double in size.

Turn out onto board and knead out bubbles. Form into 1 round or 2 long loaves and place on floured baking pan. Brush top with melted butter or margarine and pierce with a fork in several places. Let rise about 1/2 hour. Bake in 350° F oven for about an hour, or until light golden brown. Brush with water when finished baking (harder crust) or with melted butter (softer crust).

Variation: *Mrs. Raymond Vopat* submitted a similar bread recipe from the "After Harvest Czech Festival" sponsored annually by the Chamber of Commerce in Wilson, the Czech capital of Kansas. Add 1 Tbs. molasses and 2 cups rye flour with remainder in white flour for a lighter bread.

Old-Fashioned White Bread
(Made the Modern Way)
Bílý Chléb po Staru

Mrs. Emil Votroubek, Cedar Rapids, Iowa

2 1/4 cups milk (or 2 1/4 water and 2/3 cup dry milk)
3 Tbs. butter
5 to 6 cups all-purpose flour
2 pkgs. dry yeast
2 Tbs. sugar
2 tsp. salt

Heat milk and butter to 120° F. In large bowl, combine 3 cups flour, yeast, sugar, salt, and warm milk. Mix with doughmaker for 3 to 4 minutes. Gradually add enough remaining flour to form a stiff dough. Knead with dough-hooks until smooth and satiny, about 4 to 5 minutes. Dough will not be sticky to the fingers when kneaded enough. Place dough in a greased bowl; turn to grease top. Cover and let rise until double in size, about an hour. Punch down and divide into 2 parts. Shape into smooth balls, cover and let rest about 10 minutes. Shape into loaves and place in 2 greased 9" x 5" x 3" pans. Let rise until doubled, about 45 minutes. Bake in preheated oven at 375° F for 10 minutes, reduce heat to 350° F and continue to bake for 35 minutes. Remove from pans and cool on rack.

Variations:
Garlic Cheese Bread: Add 1 cup shredded Cheddar cheese and 1 tsp. garlic powder during first mixing.
Raisin Cinnamon Bread: Add 1 1/2 cups raisins and 2 tsps. cinnamon during mixing.
Onion Bread: Add 1 pkg. dry onion soup mix during first mixing. Omit salt.
Light Rye Bread: Replace 2 cups white flour with 2 cups rye flour and add 1 Tbs. caraway seeds.

Bread Sticks
Chlébové Tyčinky

Mrs. Floyd D. Herman of Wilber, Nebraska, wrote: "I am a retired farm house wife. The advent of the Wilbur Czech Festival triggered my increased interest in our family's heritage. My husband and I have 5 children. Susan was Wilber Czech Queen and Nebraska Czech Queen in 1968. Our five children are 100 percent Czech."

1 package yeast
2/3 cup warm water
1 Tbs. sugar
1 tsp. salt
2 Tbs. salad oil
2 Tbs. olive oil
2 1/4 cups flour

Soften yeast in warm water (115° F). Stir in remaining ingredients. Knead about 8 minutes. Let rise until double. Form into bread sticks the diameter of a pencil. They may be any length but if 8" this should make about 50 breadsticks. Put on greased cookie sheets. Brush breadsticks with melted lard, margarine, or beaten egg. Salt generously. Let rise approximately 30 minutes in warm place. Bake 25 to 30 minutes in a preheated 325° F oven.

The breadsticks are crisp and tender and keep fresh-tasting indefinitely.

Featherweight Pancakes
Lívance Jako Peřiccka

George Joens, owner of Joens Brothers Interiors in Czech Village, Cedar Rapids, submitted this recipe in memory of his mother, Martha Joens, of Czech descent, who inspired him to help commemorate the Czech people and their heritage. George was the first president of the Czech Village Association, in 1972.

1 cup dry bread crumbs
3 Tbs. melted butter
2 Tbs. brown sugar
1 tsp. cinnamon
2 cups milk
3 eggs, separated
1 cup flour
3 tsp. baking powder
1/2 tsp. salt

Mix together bread crumbs, butter, sugar, and cinnamon and brown in a skillet, stirring constantly. Pour 1 cup milk over mixture and let stand until milk is absorbed. In a mixing bowl, beat egg yolks and rest of milk, and stir in flour, baking powder, and salt. Mix until smooth, then add crumb mixture. Fold in stiffly beaten egg whites. Bake on hot griddle.

Grandma Kubicek's Houska
Houska dle Babicky Kubickove

Mary Jen Kubicek Bear and her husband Dick own and operate two art galleries and framing studios in Cedar Rapids, Iowa.

2 cakes yeast
1/4 cup lukewarm water
1 cup milk, scalded
1/2 cup sugar
1/2 cup butter or shortening
2 eggs
1 egg yolk
1 tsp. grated lemon rind
1/4 tsp. mace
1 1/2 tsp. salt
4 1/2 to 5 cups flour
1/2 cup raisins
1/2 cup almonds
1 cup mixed candied fruits

Dissolve yeast in water. Pour scalded milk over salt, sugar, and butter. Add eggs, lemon rind, mace, salt, 1 cup flour, and yeast mixture. Beat until smooth, adding 2 cups of flour. Let rise until double. Add raisins, almonds, and candied fruit sprinkled with a little flour. Turn onto board and knead rest of the flour into dough. Divide dough in half, then each half into thirds and form into braids. Place on greased baking sheet. Let rise until light. Combine egg white and 1 Tbs. water, brush on braids. Bake at 350° F for 30 to 35 minutes.

Czech Coffee Cake
Česká Vanočka

Emma Havlena Barta came to America at age 16, when a brother already established in Cedar Rapids sent for her. She and her husband, Joseph Barta, were founders of St. Ludmila Parish where Mr. Barta worked as a builder on the church, rectory and convent. They raised 10 children.

This recipe was also submitted by Georgiana F. Brejcha of Cedar Rapids, who spoke only Czech until she started school. After an initial course in Czech Heritage at Kirkwood, Georgiana continued her education. At age 64 she graduated from Kirkwood with a degree as a Teacher Associate.

2 1/2 cups milk, warmed
2 packages yeast
1 Tbs. sugar
2 tsp. salt
3 eggs, beaten
1 tsp. mace
1 cup sugar
1 cup butter, melted
1 cup almonds, blanched and slivered
1 cup yellow raisins, softened in warm water and drained
approximately 8 cups flour

Combine warm milk, yeast, 1 Tbs. sugar, and enough flour to make a sponge the consistency of pancake batter. Mix well, cover loosely and let rise 1/2 hour in a warm place. Stir down and add remaining ingredients, working in the flour last. Add just enough flour to make a soft dough; this may be more or less than eight cups. The almonds and raisins tend to pop out of the dough if it is too stiff. Knead 10 minutes on a heavily floured board or until the dough is shiny and elastic. Let rise until double. Punch down. Now divide to make 2, 3, or 4 loaves, or one giant *houska* can be made.

To make a single braid, cut off 1/3 of dough and set aside. Divide remaining 2/3 into 3 equal parts. Roll out the 3 pieces to approximately the same length and width. Set all three side-by-side. Form a braid by beginning in the center and working out to each end. Fold ends together and turn under. Brush with beaten egg and place on baking sheet. Repeat with remaining 1/3 of dough and set the braid firmly on top of the large one. If necessary use toothpicks or skewers to secure. Let rise until double. Bake in preheated 350° F oven. For small loaves bake 25-35 minutes, for a large one bake 1 hour. While warm, brush with melted butter. When cool, braid can be frosted with confectioner's sugar icing flavored with almond extract. Decorate with more slivered almonds, candied cherry halves, etc.

Bohemian Christmas Houska
Česká Vánočni Houska

Marjorie Hayek is a painter from Iowa City whose beautiful oils have been widely exhibited and reproduced. Reproductions of her painting of "Old Brick," a historic Iowa City church, are being sold to help finance the building's restoration. She said, "My easel and my painting sustain me." And, in this case, sustain "Old Brick."

1 cup dark raisins
1 cup white raisins
1/4 cup brandy
1 cup milk, scalded
1 cup lard
1 cup sugar
1 1/2 tsp. salt
1 cup water
1 oz. cake yeast or 2 pkgs. dry yeast, dissolved with 1 tsp. sugar and 1/4 cup warm water
2 eggs plus 1 egg yolk
1/2 cup nuts
6 1/2 cups flour

Soak raisins in brandy for 2 to 3 hours. Pour scalded milk over lard, sugar, and salt. Stir until lard is dissolved, add 1 cup water to make mixture lukewarm. Add yeast mixture, eggs, raisins, and nuts. Then add flour. Shape into loaves and bake at 350° F for one hour. May be frosted if desired.

Christmas Sweet Braids
Vánočka

Lester Sykora, Cedar Rapids, Iowa.

- 8 cups flour
- 1/4 tsp. mace
- 1/4 tsp. nutmeg
- 1 1/2 tsp. salt
- 1 tsp. dry lemon peel or grated lemon rind
- 1 cup butter
- 1 cup sugar
- 2 cups milk, heated
- 2 eggs and 2 egg yolks
- 2 envelopes dry yeast dissolved in 1/4 cup warm water with pinch of sugar
- 2 tsp. vanilla
- 1/2 cup light raisins
- 1/4 cup or more slivered almonds
- 1/2 cup candied fruit, chopped fine

Mix flour with spices and lemon rind. Work in butter as you would for pie crust. Put the cup of sugar into heated milk. Beat the eggs and 2 yolks together. When milk cools, add half the flour. Keep mixing; add beaten eggs, then yeast dissolved in the water. Add remaining flour until you have a nice, smooth dough. Then add vanilla, raisins, almonds and candied fruit. Mix well, cover, and let stand in warm place until dough rises to double. Punch down and place on lightly floured board. Divide dough into 9 parts. Roll each piece by hand into 12-inch strips. Braid 4 strips together and put on a greased pan 16 1/2" x 10". Braid 3 more strips together and place on top of the first braid. Then twist together the last 2 strips and place on top of the other 2 layers. Let rise in warm place about 35 minutes.

Egg wash:
- 1 egg
- 1 Tbs. milk
- 1 tsp. sugar

Beat egg with milk and sugar. Brush braids and bake about 1 hour in preheated 350° F oven. When cool, sprinkle with powdered sugar. This recipe will make two smaller loaves (adjust baking time to 45 mins.).

Easter Yeast Cake
Mazanec

Mrs. Frank J. Stastny of Cedar Rapids is interested in quilting and crafts. Her activities in church work, Sokol, and C.S.A. keep her busy.

- 2 cakes fresh yeast
- 1 cup lukewarm milk
- 1/2 cup butter, melted
- 2 egg yolks
- 1/4 to 1/2 cup light raisins
- 4 1/2 cups flour
- 1/2 cup sugar
- 1 tsp. salt
- 1/2 tsp. grated lemon peel
- 1 tsp. vanilla
- 1/3 cup almonds, finely chopped

Place yeast in a bowl, sprinkle with 1 Tbs. sugar and stir until yeast and sugar are like a liquid. Add 2 Tbs. flour and 2 Tbs. warm milk. Mix well. Cover with cloth and let rise in a warm place 5 to 10 minutes. Add the rest of ingredients and beat with a wooden spoon until thoroughly blended. Turn onto floured pastry board and knead until dough is not sticky. Place back in bowl, lightly oil top, cover with cloth and let rise in a warm place until dough is doubled. Then shape dough on lightly floured board into one large round loaf or two smaller round loaves. Place on well greased baking sheet and brush with one beaten whole egg. Sprinkle with more chopped almonds. Cut a cross in the top of each round with scissors. Let rise a bit longer and bake in a 400° F oven 15 minutes. Reduce heat to 375° F and bake 30 to 45 minutes more, depending on whether you are baking two rounds or one.

Kolaches

Kolaches
Koláče

Genevieve Wombacher of Iowa City offers her recipe which has won five blue ribbons at the state fair. "I have been baking kolaches ever since I was old enough to bake. My mother and dad, Mr. and Mrs. Ed Hradek, were full-blooded Bohemians, so I have always been with that kind of cooking and baking and love it very much." She is also manager of the lunch program at Regina High School.

3 pkgs. dry yeast dissolved in 1/2 cup lukewarm water with 1 Tbs. sugar
2 cups milk
1/2 cup sugar
1 Tbs. salt
1/2 cup shortening, oleo or butter
3 egg yolks, and 1 whole egg, beaten
5 to 6 cups flour

Dissolve yeast and sugar in lukewarm water and set aside to work. Scald milk and let cool to lukewarm, then add sugar, salt, melted shortening, and beaten eggs. Mix well, then beat in 3 cups of flour. Add yeast mixture and mix well. Then add enough flour to make a soft dough. After dough is mixed well, place in greased bowl and let rise until double. Make balls of dough and put on greased cookie sheet. Let rise. When raised, push centers of balls down and fill with filling of your choice. Let rise again and bake at 400° F until brown, about 7 minutes. Grease tops when taken from oven, and place on rack to cool. Makes 5 dozen.

Cherry, pineapple, apricot, prune and poppy seed are favorite fillings. A little applesauce mixed with the prune not only helps "stretch it" but also tends to mellow the flavor.

Kolache Dainties
Koláčky

Vilma Nejdl of Ely, Iowa, is active in the Cedar Rapids Sokol and is the manager of their colorful Beseda Dancers.

2 pkgs. yeast
1/2 cup coffee cream, warmed
2 Tbs. sugar
4 cups flour
3/4 pound butter
6 egg yolks, beaten
1/4 tsp. mace
1/4 tsp. salt
1/2 tsp. grated lemon rind

Dissolve yeast in lukewarm cream, add sugar, and set aside to rise. Put flour into bowl and cut in butter until mixture is crumbly. Add beaten egg yolks to yeast mixture, add spices and lemon rind and add all to crumb mixture and beat until dough is stiff and smooth. Cover and place in refrigerator overnight. The next day, roll out dough 1/4-inch thick and cut into small squares, approximately 2 inches. Fill with choice of filling. Brush each corner with beaten egg, bring corners together and seal securely. Brush tops of the kolaches with beaten egg, place on ungreased pan, bake 10 to 12 minutes at 400° F. Yields 6 1/2 to 7 dozen.

A Poppy Seed Story

Paul Engle, noted American poet and writer, remembers that the Cedar Rapids Czechs were great wine makers. During Prohibition, they made even more. When he was a newsboy selling the Cedar Rapids *Gazette,* many of the newsboys were Czech, and they all enjoyed buying poppy seed kolaches at the Sykora bakery.

"My mother did not want me to eat any poppy seed kolaches so that I would not acquire the opium habit. Naturally, I ate every one I could get my hands on. To this day, I have still not acquired the opium habit."

Kolaches
Koláče

Helen Horak Nemec grew up near Czech Village, Cedar Rapids, and has worked at Sykora's Bakery. Helen's father came to America following World War I, then sent for her mother after he had found a job. Everyone spoke Czech in Helen's household so she did not learn English until she went to school. "My mother made buchty *(covered kolaches). I ate the top of the kolache first and put the poppy seed with the bottom down, and my brothers would always steal it from me!"*

2 pkgs. dry yeast
1/4 cup lukewarm water
1 Tbs. sugar
1 cup butter or margarine
2 cups milk
2 whole eggs, and 4 yolks
1/2 cup sugar
1/2 tsp. mace
1 1/2 tsp. salt
1/2 tsp. grated lemon rind
6 to 7 cups flour

Dissolve yeast in lukewarm water, add 1 Tbs. sugar and let set until bubbly. Melt butter and add 2 cups milk, heat until warm. Beat the eggs and yolks and add sugar, beating until eggs and sugar become thick. Add warm milk with melted butter. Add yeast, mace, salt, and lemon rind. Next beat in flour 1 cup at a time. When dough becomes too thick to beat with spoon, turn out on floured board and knead until smooth and silky. Put in greased bowl and let rise in warm place until double. Turn dough onto lightly floured board and divide into 6 large pieces. Cut each of these into 12 small pieces. Form into walnut size balls. (form with your palm.) Place on greased baking sheet 2 inches apart and brush each ball with butter. Let rise until almost double in size. Press center and fill with filling. Let rise until light. Bake at 400° F about 7-10 minutes. Brush kolaches with butter after you take them from the oven. Makes about 6 dozen.

Crumb Topping for Kolaches
Kolačová Posýpka

1 cup flour
1/2 cup sugar
1/4 cup butter or margarine
1/4 tsp. salt (omit if using margarine)
1/4 tsp. cinnamon

Mix all ingredients together, (using a pastry blender) until crumbly. Use as a topping for kolaches or coffee cakes.

Cherry Filling
Višňová Nádivka

1 cup sugar
6 Tbs. cornstarch
1/4 tsp. salt
2 cans red sour cherries
1 tsp. red food coloring
1 tsp. vanilla
1/2 tsp. almond flavoring

Mix sugar, cornstarch and salt. Add juice from cherries. Cook and stir until thick. Add remaining ingredients. Makes enough filling for 3 dozen kolaches.

Poppy Seed Filling
Maková Nádivka

1/2 pound ground poppy seed
1 cup water
1 cup milk
1 Tbs. butter
1 tsp. vanilla
1/2 tsp. cinnamon
1 cup sugar
1/2 cup crushed graham crackers
1/2 cup softened raisins

Add water to ground poppy seed and cook until thickened. Add milk and cook slowly for about 10 minutes, being careful that it does not scorch. Add butter, vanilla, and cinnamon, then sugar and continue cooking for about 5 minutes and remove from burner. Add graham cracker crumbs and raisins. Makes enough filling for 3 dozen kolaches.

Scones
Nadívané Vdolečky

This recipe was submitted by Mary Ann and Stanley Studenka on behalf of the membership of the Czech Dancers Polka Club of Metamora, Ohio. The Polka Club was formed in 1970, to promote Czech and Moravian traditions. Dance groups perform in traditional costumes, accompanied by push-button accordionists. At the biggest event of the year, held on the first Sunday in August, pastries are served. These recipes have been handed down by the Studenkas' mothers and grandmothers.

2 cups half-and-half
1/2 cup sugar
2 packages yeast
8 egg yolks, at room temperature
1/2 pound butter, softened at room temperature
6 cups flour, more or less, as needed

Heat half-and-half to lukewarm. Add sugar and yeast and let sit until dissolved (about 10 minutes). Beat egg yolks; add soft butter and blend. Mix in flour, and knead until dough is smooth and satiny and does not stick to a wooden spoon. Cover and let rise until double. Punch down and spoon out dough pieces the size of a walnut. Flatten each piece and add favorite filling. Bring sides over filling and seal well. Place sealed side down, on lightly greased pan, about 1 inch apart. Let rise slightly; then brush with egg yolk mixed with a little milk. Sprinkle with streusel topping. Bake at 350° F until nicely browned, 12-15 minutes. Makes 85.

Poppy Seed Filling
Makovaá Nápiň

1/2 lb. ground poppy seed
1/2 cup sugar
3 Tbs. milk
1/4 tsp. cinnamon – optional
2 Tbs. butter, melted

Combine all ingredients; stir and cook over low heat about 5 minutes. Cool. Use 1/2 tsp. for each pastry.

Prune Filling (or Peach or Apricot)
Švestková – Broskvová Nebo Meruňkova Nápiň

2 lbs. dried prunes, peaches or apricots
1 cup sugar
1 tsp. vanilla

Cook dried fruit in enough water to cover until tender. Drain, pit, and mash well. Add sugar and vanilla and mix well.

Nut Filling
Ořechová Nápiň

4 egg whites
1 1/4 cups sugar
1/8 tsp. salt
1/2 pound ground walnuts

Stiffly beat egg whites. Combine sugar, salt, and walnuts; then fold into egg whites. Fill pastry with 1/2 tsp. each.

Cottage Cheese Filling
Tvarohavá Nápiň

1 Tbs. butter
1 lb. dried sweet cottage cheese
1 egg yolk
1/4 cup raisins
1/2 cup sugar
1/4 tsp. salt
1/4 tsp. vanilla or lemon flavor

Mix all ingredients together well. Do not prepare until ready to use.

Streusel Topping
Posýoka

3 Tbs. flour
1/2 tsp. vanilla
5 Tbs. sugar
3 Tbs. butter

Mix all ingredients together with fingers until crumb-like. Sprinkle over top of scones before baking.

Desserts

Poppy Seed Cake
Maková Buchta

In the early 1900's Lester Sykora's father came to America and operated a grocery and bakery in Cedar Rapids and one in Long Prairie, Minnesota. In 1927 he purchased and founded the Sykora Bakery as it is today in the Czech Village. "My father incorporated a lot of the baking recipes his mother used in Bohemia into his formulas which we still use, especially our Bohemian Rye Bread and kolaches. It was a family project, Mom, Dad, and us 4 kids, for some 40 years. My sister Elsie Elias and myself are left."

1/3 cup poppy seed
1 cup buttermilk
1 cup margarine
1 1/2 cups sugar
4 eggs
1 orange rind, grated
1/2 tsp. vanilla
1/2 tsp. salt
2 1/2 cups sifted flour
2 tsp. baking powder
1 tsp. soda
2 Tbs. granulated sugar and
   2 tsp. cinnamon, blended

Soak poppy seed in buttermilk overnight. Cream margarine and sugar until smooth. Beat in eggs one at a time. Stir in vanilla, salt, and grated orange rind. Sift flour, baking powder and soda together and add alternately with soaked poppy seed and milk. Mix to a smooth batter. Pour 1/2 batter into either a 10" angel food or bundt pan, which has been greased and floured. Sprinkle cinnamon sugar mix on batter, then add rest of batter. Bake at 350° F for 35 minutes, or until a toothpick inserted into the middle comes out clean.

Poppy Seed Cake
Maková Buchta

Beth Kouba, Yukon, Oklahoma

3 cups flour
2 cups sugar
1 1/2 cups salad oil
4 eggs
1 tsp. vanilla
1/2 tsp. salt
1 1/2 tsp. baking soda
1 (14-ounce) can evaporated milk
1 jar poppy seed filling
1 cup pecans, chopped

Mix all ingredients until smooth. Beat well with electric mixer on medium speed for 2 minutes. Bake for 1 hour and 10 minutes in ungreased 10" tube pan, at 350° F. Cool cake before removing from pan.

Poppy Seed Coffee Cake
Maková Babovka

Helen Horak Nemec, Cedar Rapids, Iowa

1 package dry yeast
1/4 cup warm water
1 cup milk
1/2 cup sugar
1/2 cup shortening
1/2 tsp. salt
2 eggs, beaten
3 or more cups of flour

Dissolve yeast in warm water and set aside until bubbly. Scald the milk, add sugar, shortening, and salt. Cool to lukewarm and add the beaten eggs, yeast mixture, and flour. Knead until the dough looks satiny. Place in greased bowl and let rise until double. Turn out onto floured board and roll out 1/2 inch thick. Spread with poppy seed filling (see kolache recipes). Roll like jelly roll, crimp edges together and put into greased Bundt or angel food cake pan. Grease top, let rise until double. Bake 1 hour at 325° F.

Christmas Poppy Seed Cake
Vánoční Maková Buchta

Fern Kaplan Fackler, Cedar Rapids, discovered this poppy seed cake recipe when her children were small. "I always looked forward to Christmas time when I was growing up as the food was so delicious, and we were treated to several kinds of baked goods with poppy seed. My daughter decided that we should have our own Christmas tradition and have this cake for Christmas morning. We have continued the poppy seed tradition for many years."

12 ounces poppy seed filling
1 cup margarine
1 1/2 cups sugar
4 eggs separated
1 tsp. vanilla
1 cup sour cream
1 Tbs. mayonnaise
2 1/2 cups sifted flour
1 tsp. soda

Cream margarine and 1 cup of sugar together. Add poppy seed filling, and egg yolks one at a time. Blend in vanilla, sour cream, and mayonnaise. Sift flour and soda together and add slowly to poppy seed mixture. Beat egg whites until stiff, slowly adding 1/2 cup of sugar. Beat well, then fold into poppy seed mixture. Pour into greased tube cake pan which has bottom lined with waxed paper. Bake at 350° F for 1 hour and 15 to 20 minutes. Cool 5 minutes before removing from pan, peel off waxed paper. Sift powdered sugar onto top of cake through a doily or paper cutout.

Poppy Seed Filling
Maková Nápiň

Commercial poppy seed filling may be used or the following recipe.

1 pound ground poppy seed
4 cups water
1 cup milk
1 1/2 cups sugar
2 Tbs. vanilla
2 Tbs. butter

Cook poppy seed and water 10 to 15 minutes. Add milk and cook another 10 to 15 minutes. When done add sugar, vanilla, and butter. This may be frozen when not needed right away. Use 1 1/2 cups in the above recipe.

Nut Coffee Cake
Ořechová Bábovka

Marjorie Kopecek Nejdl of Cedar Rapids enjoys painting the beautiful Czech Easter eggs.

5 cups flour
2 packages dry yeast
1/2 cup sugar
1 1/3 cups warm milk
1/2 cup butter, melted
1 tsp. vanilla extract
1 tsp. grated lemon rind
2 eggs, slightly beaten
1/2 tsp. salt

Sift the flour into a large bowl and make a well in the middle. Put in yeast, 1 Tbs. sugar and 1/2 cup warm milk. Let stand for 10 minutes. Add remaining milk and ingredients. Mix then beat well with a wooden spoon until smooth. Cover and let rise in a warm place until double in size (about 1 1/2 hours). On a floured board, roll out dough to 1/4- 1/2-inch thickness. Spread nut filling on the dough and roll as for a jelly roll. Place in a well greased *babovka* (or Bundt pan) and let rise for another 1 1/2 hours. Bake in preheated 350° F oven for about 45 minutes. Let cool about 5 minutes, then invert onto a plate and powder with powdered sugar before serving.

Nut Filling

1/2 cup sugar
1/4 cup butter, melted
1 tsp. vanilla
2 eggs, separated
1 1/2 cups finely ground nuts

Cream sugar, butter, vanilla, and egg yolks. Beat well. Beat egg whites separately until stiff, fold into butter mixture. Fold in nuts.

Bessie's Apple Strudel
Jablkový Závin

This recipe is from Konecny's Restaurant which has been a traditional family style establishment with its "down home" cooking for the past 30 years in Cedar Rapids. The menu varies with the entrées, as well as the soups and desserts, all made from scratch. One special entrée offered every Friday is Konecny's famous Fried Turtle.

1/4 cup butter, melted
1/4 cup milk, warm
1/4 tsp. salt
1 egg, well beaten
1 1/4 cups plus 2 level Tbs. flour
4 cups peeled and sliced apples
1 Tbs. butter
1/3 cup raisins
3/4 cup sugar
1/4 cup nuts

Mix melted butter, milk, salt, egg, and flour together and place in a well-floured bowl. Cover and keep warm while preparing apples. Place dough mixture on well-floured pastry cloth and stretch with your hands until pulled paper thin. Spread apples on dough. Mix butter, raisins, sugar and nuts and sprinkle over the apples. Roll up like a jelly roll and place on a greased cookie sheet. Seam side down. Brush top of roll with 1 tsp. butter or cream. Bake at 375° F for 30 minutes, then reduce heat to 350° F and continue baking until apples are tender. Baste the top with its own syrup, to which may be added a small amount of cream, to keep the strudel from getting a hard crust. Yields 24 servings.

Angel Pie
Andělský Dort

Janelle Votroubek McClain and her husband George are the proprietors of an art gallery and frame studio in Cedar Rapids. They gave a painting by Zora DuVall, artist of Czechoslovakian descent, to the Czech Heritage Museum in Cedar Rapids. Janelle writes of this recipe: "At Christmas time I like to decorate this with red and green maraschino cherries cut to look like poinsettias."

1 cup milk
1/2 cup sugar
2 Tbs. flour
2 eggs whites
dash of salt
1 tsp. vanilla or almond flavoring
1 pie shell, baked
1 cup heavy cream, whipped

Cook milk, sugar, and flour together until thick; cool. Beat egg whites until stiff and fold into the pudding. Add flavoring. Pour into baked pie shell or crumb shell. Cover with whipped cream. Refrigerate 3 to 4 hours. May be frozen.

Great-Grandma Kubicek's Rhubarb Custard Pie
Reveňový Nakyp Prababičky Kubíčkové

Margaret Z. Kubicek, Cedar Rapids, Iowa

1 recipe plain pastry (below)
1 1/2 to 2 cups sugar
3 Tbs. flour
1/8 tsp. salt
2 eggs, beaten
3 cups rhubarb, cut in pieces

Combine sugar, flour, and salt. Add eggs, beating until smooth. Stir in rhubarb. Fill 9-inch pastry lined pan. Adjust top crust. Bake at 450° F for 10 minutes, then at 350° F for 30 minutes.

Plain Pastry:
2 cups flour
1 tsp. salt
2/3 cup shortening
5 to 6 Tbs. cold water

Sift flour and salt. Cut in shortening until mixture is size of small peas. Slowly add water, mix and press ingredients together until dough holds together. Divide and roll on lightly floured surface to make 2 crusts.

Nice and Easy Nut Roll
Chutné a Jednoduché Ořechové Rohlíčky

Submitted by Mary Ann and Stanley Studenka on behalf of the Czech Dancers Polka Club, Metamora, Ohio.

2 pkgs. dry yeast
1/2 cup milk, warmed
6 cups flour
3 Tbs. sugar
1 Tbs. salt
2 cups butter
1 cup sour cream
3 eggs, beaten

In small bowl, dissolve yeast in warm milk, set aside. In large bowl combine flour, sugar, salt, butter, sour cream, and eggs. Beat well. Add yeast and milk mixture and blend well. Divide dough into four equal parts. (Divide each again for smaller rolls.) Roll into thin oblongs and spread with nut mixture. Roll up, lightly sealing edges. Place on greased baking sheet and let rise until double. Bake at 350° F for 30-40 minutes.

Nut Filling
Ořechová Nápiň

4 egg whites
1/4 cup sugar
1/8 tsp. salt
1/2 pound walnuts, ground

Beat egg whites until stiff. Combine sugar, salt, and walnuts, then fold into egg whites. Fill pastry.

Apple Bublanina
Jablková "Bublanina"

Arlene and Jerry Boddicker own the Boddicker School of Music in the Czech Village. Arlene, who collects old-time band arrangements for the Boddicker band, also teaches at Coe College and Mt. Mercy College in Cedar Rapids.

"This recipe has been handed down for four generations on my mother's side of the family. Grandma Buresh to Grandma Hiroutek to Aunt Emma Zbanek to me."

3 quarts apples, peeled and sliced
1 1/2 cups sugar
1 tsp. cinnamon or more
1/2 cup margarine or butter
2 eggs
2 cups milk
1 Tbs. sugar
2/3 tsp. salt
2 cups flour
1 tsp. baking powder

Place apples, 1 1/2 cups sugar, and cinnamon in large bowl. Mix and set aside. Melt margarine in 9"x13"x2" cake pan. Beat eggs until blended, add milk, 1 Tbs. sugar, and salt. Add flour and baking powder, making a thick batter, then pour over apples. Mix well and pour into cake pan, patting down firmly with back of spoon. As butter rises around edge of pan, dip up with spoon and spread over top of batter. Bake at 350° F for 1 hour and 15 minutes or until apples are golden. Serve warm or cold with whipped cream or ice cream. Serves 18.

Cherry Bublanina
Třešňová "Bublanina"

Arlene Boddicker was given this recipe by her cousin, Agnes Konicek.

1/2 cup butter
1/2 cup sugar
3 eggs, separated
1 cup flour
1/2 tsp. baking powder
pinch of salt
1 quart cherries, pitted (fresh, canned, or frozen), well drained

Cream together butter and sugar. Beat egg yolks until lemon colored. Add butter and sugar, beat until fluffy. Sift flour, baking powder, and salt together, then add to butter mixture. Beat egg whites until stiff and fold into batter slowly. Pour into greased 12"x8" pan. Sprinkle cherries over top of the batter, do not mix. Bake at 450° F for 15 minutes.

Divine Crullers
Boží Milosti

M. Melvina Svec of Cedar Rapids remembers that these have also been called Listi *(leaves)* and Krapace *(crispies)*.

1 egg
1 1/3 cups flour
1 Tbs. water
fat for deep frying

Combine egg and water, beating well. Add flour as needed until dough is similar to noodle dough. Amount of flour will vary with the size of the egg. Turn dough onto cloth or board and knead using rest of flour. Cut dough into 3 or 4 chunks. Roll out each piece as thin as possible, cut into pieces 2" to 3" across–squares, rectangles, triangles or any shapes to use the dough. Cut a diagonal slash in each piece. To test if fat is hot enough, drop a sample piece in; it should rise to the surface at once. As pieces are dropped into the fat, push fork through the slash to keep it open. When the slash is lightly brown, turn the piece over. Two forks may be helpful as one must work fast. Lift pieces onto brown paper to drain. When cooled sprinkle with powdered sugar if served at once. Otherwise store in tight container and sugar them just before serving. Makes about 2 dozen. They enlarge during frying. This recipe does not include milk, cream, flavoring, salt, or butter.

Celestial Crusts
Boží Milosti

Esther Hronik Klersey was born in the heart of Czech Village when board sidewalks and dirt roads were common, and that area is very dear to her. As with her father, music has been her life. Most notably she directed the Karla Masaryk Chorus (named for the wife of the first president of Czechoslovakia), which dressed in authentic Czech costumes and appeared with many celebrities. They also recorded for the "Voice of America."

3 eggs
3 tsp. sugar
2 Tbs. butter or lard
1/2 egg shell of water or cream
dash of salt
flour

Mix eggs, sugar, butter, cream, salt, and enough flour to make a stiff dough (but not as stiff as for noodles). Work all ingredients into a smooth dough. On lightly floured board, roll dough very thin. Cut into 3" squares and prick with a fork several times. Fry in deep fat, like doughnuts, until lightly browned on both sides. Remove from fat and drain on paper towel. Dust generously with powdered sugar.

Divine Crullers
Boží Milosti

Irma and John Kadlec have worked together in a car distributorship in Czech Village for many years.

4 egg yolks, well beaten
4 Tbs. heavy cream
2 Tbs. sugar
1 egg white, beaten stiff
2 Tbs. rum or whiskey
1/8 tsp. salt
1 3/4 to 2 cups flour

Beat egg yolks, cream and sugar until well blended. Fold in egg white and rum or whiskey. Add salt and 1 cup flour, mix well. Add remaining flour gradually, mixing until dough is stiff. Knead for a minute and roll out 1/8" thick. Cut into strips about 1 1/2" x 4". Slash edges and twist slightly. Drop into hot deep fat at 360° F and fry until golden brown. Drain and dust with powdered sugar. Makes about 3 dozen.

Czech Tradition

City or town squares were used in the evening hours as promenades for local people and especially young lovers.

Cream Puffs and Filling
Lehké Pečivo s Nápiňí

Leona Melhus of Atkins, Iowa, came from a family of 8 children and started working at 12 years of age. She is a well-known cook in the Cedar Rapids Czech community, and works at Joens Brothers Interiors in Czech Village.

1 cup water
1/2 cut butter or margarine
1 cup flour
4 eggs

Bring butter and water to a boil, add flour and cook until dough leaves sides of pan, about 1 minute. Remove from heat. Add eggs one at a time, beat thoroughly. Drop by tablespoonfuls on cookie sheet. Bake at 425° F for 20 minutes, then 325° F for 25 to 30 minutes. Makes 18. Cool before filling.

Filling:

2/3 cups sugar
1/2 tsp. salt
2 1/2 tsp. cornstarch
1 Tbs. flour
3 cups milk
3 eggs, separated
2 Tbs. butter
2 tsp. vanilla

Mix sugar, salt, cornstarch, and flour, add milk and cook in double boiler until slightly thickened. Add small amount of hot mixture to egg yolks and return to hot mixture, cook until thick. Remove from heat and add vanilla and butter. Chill. Beat egg whites thick with 1 Tbs. sugar. Fold into cream mixture. Slice puffs horizontally and place a tablespoonful of filling into each.

Mother's Chocolate Fudge
Maminčino Čokoládové Cukroví

Hedrika Konecny Benesh of Cedar Rapids writes of her mother, Mrs. Adloph (Anna) Vavara Konecny. "Mother was born in Czechoslovakia and helped raise twin baby brothers after her mother's death. At the age of fourteen she came to Cedar Rapids, with the aid of an older brother who had come earlier, and worked in the Grand Hotel, where she met and married our father. They moved to a farm near Ely, where they raised practically everything they needed, and even made cheese and butter to sell. Dad cured and smoked hams and bacon for himself and for the neighbors. Mother would fry down pork, make jaternice, jelita, *and also* presburt.

"Holiday dinners would always include roast duck or goose, sage dressing, sauerkraut, potato dumplings and pumpkin pie. At Christmas there was houska, *a variety of cookies, as well as* bozi milosit. *There were always* kolaches, rohlicky, *and delicious chicken on Sunday. Rye bread was baked during the week, as well as pies. How she did it and took care of a large garden, helped with the harvest of the fields, washing, ironing, and all is hard to realize. Especially when you realize that all the water was carried in from the well and the firewood for the cookstove, too. But what delicious meals were served. Nuts and dried apples were more delicacies we had to nibble on. Mushrooms were also dried or canned for winter along with all the fruits and vegetables. Winter evenings would be spent reading or ladies got together to strip feathers. They enjoyed visiting while working and a lunch would always follow."

2 cups brown sugar
1 cup heavy cream
3/4 cup corn syrup
2 squares bitter chocolate
pinch salt
1 cup (or more) black walnuts
1 tsp. vanilla

Boil together the sugar, cream, corn syrup, salt and chocolate, until a few drops form a soft ball when dropped in cold water. Remove from heat and cool. Add vanilla and beat. Add nuts and beat until stiff. Pour quickly into a buttered loaf cake pan. Let cool and cut into squares. Mother used plenty of nuts, probably 3 or 3 1/2 cups. This is not so sweet as most candies.

Christmas Pudding Candy
Vánoční Mekké Cukroví

Mrs. Stanley Rejcha of Beatrice, Nebraska, sent a recipe of her great grandmother's, which she makes in November to be ready for Christmas.

3 cups sugar
1 cup cream
1 Tbs. butter
1 tsp. vanilla
1 pound dates, cut up
1 pound figs, cut up
1 pound raisins
1 pound shredded coconut
1 cup nuts, chopped

Cook sugar, cream and butter to soft ball stage–234° F. Beat until creamy. Beat in vanilla, fruit and nuts. Roll up like a cookie roll and wrap in a damp cloth, then in waxed paper, and put in a cool place to ripen. Cut in slices as needed.

Czech Garnets
České Granáty

Barbara Sovern of Cedar Rapids received this recipe from Emily Polacek, wife of an owner of The Polacek Brothers Meat Market. Barbara's father had a wholesale meat business in Chicago. One of his customers was the Polacek Brothers Meat Market, complete with sawdust on the floor.

1/2 pound butter
1 cup sugar
2 egg yolks
2 cups flour
1 cup chopped nuts
1/2 cup raspberry or strawberry jam

Cream butter and sugar. Add egg yolks and blend well. Add flour gradually, mixing thoroughly. Fold in chopped nuts. Grease 8" square pan and spoon in half of batter. Top with jam and spoon on rest of batter. Bake in 325° F oven for 1 hour. When cool, cut in small squares. Makes 3 dozen cookies.

Apple Fritters
Jabikové Smaženky

Helen Sysel Kupka is of Crete, Nebraska. "Like many early settlers, encouraged by the government, my father had an orchard of various kinds of apples. We frequently made Apple Fritters. Many cooks used lard instead of butter for frying. Present day oil for frying would be good too."

3 or 4 firm apples
powdered sugar
2 eggs, beaten
1 tsp. butter, melted
1 Tbs. milk
1 Tbs. sugar
pinch of salt
flour

Peel the apples, then slice them crosswise about 1/3" thick. Carefully remove cores. Sprinkle with powdered sugar, set aside. Mix eggs, butter, milk, sugar, salt, and enough flour to make a thin batter. Dip apple slices individually and fry in hot butter until tender and light brown.

Czechoslovakian Sugar Cookies
Česko-slovenské Cukrové Koláčky

Lenore Topinka of Cedar Rapids, Iowa

1 cup margarine
1 cup shortening
1 cup powdered sugar
1 cup granulated sugar
2 eggs
1 tsp. vanilla
1 tsp. soda
1 tsp. cream of tartar
4 cups flour

Cream margarine, shortening and sugars. Add eggs and vanilla. Stir in remaining ingredients. Roll dough into balls about the size of walnuts and roll the balls in some powdered sugar. Place on a greased cookie sheet 2-inches apart. Bake at 375° F for 12 minutes. Makes 6 dozen.

Czechoslovakian Cut-Out Cookies
Česko-slovenské Vykrajované Koláčky

Mrs. Joe (Evelyn Svoboda) Stjskal of Cedar Rapids has many fond childhood memories of growing up on a farm. "The week of Christmas we would do all the Christmas baking and Dad would take us into the timber to cut our tree. We would help him cut it down and usually hauled it on the horse-drawn sleigh. We decorated it with many pretty decorations that our mother brought from Czechoslovakia. We would put clip candle holders on the tree and Christmas Eve we'd all stand around the tree and light those wax candles for a few minutes and watch them carefully while we sang Christmas songs.

"Our trips to Cedar Rapids are also fondly remembered. Our parents would deliver their farm products, which usually consisted of dressed poultry, eggs, cream, and many other items. Then we would go on to 16th Avenue to do our grocery shopping. We would always go to Polehna's Meat Market and buy 50 cents worth of New England ham and to Sykora's Bakery to buy 25 cents worth of rolls and then return to our car to eat lunch. That was a real treat."

1 cup butter
3/4 cup powdered sugar
4 egg yolks
3 Tbs. light cream
1/2 tsp. salt
1 tsp. vanilla or lemon extract
3 cups sifted flour

Cream butter and sugar. Beat in egg yolks, cream, salt, and flavoring. Gradually stir in flour then chill for 1 hour. Roll out on board sprinkled with equal parts of flour and powdered sugar. When about 1/4" thick, cut into desired shapes and place on ungreased cookie sheet. Bake at 350° F to 375° F about 12 minutes. Cool and frost with icing.

Icing:
2 egg yolks
1 Tbs. water
1/2 tsp. flavoring
powdered sugar

Beat egg yolks and water. Add your choice of flavoring and enough powdered sugar to make spreading consistency. Frost cookies and top with chopped almonds or colored sugar.

Molasses-Ginger Bars
Perník

M. Melvina Svec is the author of My Czech Word Book: ABC Color Book. *She is the editor of the Czech Heritage Foundation's newsletter and is currently working on an album of Czech and Slovak folk and patriotic songs. She also is active as a lecturer to tourists and groups in the Cedar Rapids community.*

"Sweets were never an everyday item on the table at meals, in Old Bohemia for the average family. Even kolaches were made for festive events and special happenings. As a child we had special noodle soup and kolaches on Sunday only."

3/4 cup lard
1/2 cup sugar
1 cup molasses
1 egg
1/2 cup hot water
1 tsp. soda
3 cups flour
1 tsp. ginger
pinch salt

Cream lard and sugar together. Add molasses and blend, then add egg. Dissolve soda in hot water and let cool. Add flour, ginger, and salt alternately with soda water. Dough is rather stiff. Spread on well greased and floured 9" x 13" pan. Bake at 350° F for 20 to 25 minutes. Drizzle with thin powdered sugar frosting (powdered sugar and milk or cream beaten together) when removed from oven. Cool and cut into bars or squares.

And More

Cottage Cheese
Jak Dělat Tvaroh

Charles E. Krejci of Cedar Rapids writes, "Both my paternal and maternal grandparents migrated from Czechoslovakia. My father was born in Pilsen and came to the United States with his parents at the age of 14. My father was a carpenter by trade. My mother was born in Yankton, South Dakota and was an excellent cook and seamstress. Our family of seven lived and grew up near Riverside Park in Cedar Rapids, which together with 16th Avenue was the extent of our world. Our only foray across the 16th Avenue Bridge was to the Olympic Theatre or ZCBJ and CSPS Halls, and that was not very often."

Mrs. Krejci submits to us her cottage cheese recipe, "We ate the dry curds softened with rich milk or cream. Sometimes we added chives or onion tops. The pigs got the whey!"

Whole milk was allowed to set for 6 or 8 hours, then the cream was skimmed off and the milk used for cottage cheese. A two gallon stoneware crock was filled and set on the back of the cookstove–very little heat. The crock was covered with just any old lid. It remained there until curds developed, maybe 8 hours, maybe 24. We used a wooden spoon to stir and test. When it was ready, it was poured into a white flour sack. The whey drained off and the curds were forced into a corner of the sack and hung on the clothes line to dry for 6 to 8 hours.

Dill Gravy
Koprová Omáčka

Elsie Sykora Elias has been involved in the Sykora family bakery in Czech Village, Cedar Rapids, for more than 50 years. "Living on a small acreage, our family could use all we could grow. A late spring frost one year pretty well wiped out our berry and apple crops. Looking for a substitute, my mother made use of a bumper garden crop and surprised us one day with carrot-filled kolaches. I have to admit, they never became my 'favorite fruit,' but they took up the slack that winter. I wonder how many of our treasured recipes may have been more or less born of necessity like those carrot kolaches."

2 cups water, 1 cup may be beef broth
1 cup sour cream
2 Tbs. flour
salt, dill, and vinegar, to taste

Bring water to a boil. Mix sour cream with the flour and slowly add to the boiling water. Stir and cook just until smooth. Add dill, vinegar, and salt. Mix well and remove quickly from fire. Serve immediately as it tends to curdle if reheated.

Tomato Gravy
Rajská Omáčka

Mrs. Julia Davis and her husband own a barber shop in Czech Village, Cedar Rapids, Iowa.

5 small tomatoes
1 cup beef broth or water
3 Tbs. sugar
1/2 tsp. salt
1 tsp. cinnamon
1/4 tsp. allspice
1/4 tsp. cloves
3 Tbs. butter
3 Tbs. flour

Peel tomatoes and cook; then strain to remove the seeds or put through a blender to purée. Add the broth or water and rest of the ingredients, except the flour and butter. Make a brown roux of the flour and butter, then add the tomato mixture.

Cream Sauce
Smetanová Omáčka

Rose Kopecky, Cedar Rapids, Iowa

2 Tbs. butter
1 Tbs. flour
1/2 cup stock
1/2 cup sour cream
salt

Melt the butter and blend with flour. Gradually dilute with warmed stock (meat or vegetable). Add cream, salt to taste, mix well. Simmer gently 5 to 10 minutes.

Mushroom Fritters
Houboveé Žakusky

Mrs. Lumir Kopecky, Cedar Rapids, Iowa

1/2 pound mushrooms, chopped
1 Tbs. butter or margarine
2 eggs, separated
2 Tbs. milk
1 cup flour
1 tsp. baking powder
1/2 tsp. salt
pinch of paprika
frying oil
cream sauce

Sauté the mushrooms lightly in butter. In separate bowl beat the 2 egg yolks with milk and blend in flour, baking powder, salt and paprika. Beat the batter until smooth and add mushrooms. Beat the egg whites until stiff and fold into the batter. Drop by spoonfuls into hot oil and fry on both sides until golden brown. Serve with cream sauce.

Sauerkraut Crackers
Zelníky

Sidonia Klimesh, Spillville, Iowa, states, "This recipe came from my mother, Mrs. Mary E. Klimesh, and is in our church cookbook, except I revised it a bit. Mother will celebrate her 100th birthday June 22, 1981. She had 8 children to raise after my dad died when I was 11 and my youngest brother was one. The Zelniky are by-products of the old butchering days, when nothing was wasted. The cracklings are the residue, so to speak, after the lard has been rendered. Neighbors and friends exchanged samples to see whose jaternice, burty, and sultz (sausages) were the best."

1 cup cracklings, ground
1 cup flour, sifted
1 cup sauerkraut, partially drained
2 Tbs. sugar
1 Tbs. caraway seed

Snip the sauerkraut with kitchen shears, then add sugar, caraway seed, flour, and cracklings. Mix well and chill. Roll out a bit thicker than pie crust. Cut into 2" squares, bake on ungreased pans at 350° F until brown and crisp.

Crackling Crackers
Škvarkové Placky

Mrs. Marie Klima teaches Czech classes in the Cuba, Kansas area. The Klima family of six growing boys enjoy this recipe with coffee. "After you have made this once, you may adjust the ingredients. Grandma had no measurements. It was a pinch of this and a handful of that."

1 cup cracklings
1 tsp. salt
pinch of ginger
milk
1 cup flour

With a rolling pin, roll out the cracklings to crush as fine as possible. Place cracklings into a bowl, add salt, ginger, and flour. Add enough milk to make a soft dough. If necessary add more flour to knead smooth. Roll out to about the thickness of one's little finger and place onto a baking sheet. Brown in a moderate oven. When baked, the *placka* is broken into serving sized pieces.

This Czech snack food might also be called "pancakes with cracklings."

Sweet Popcorn
Sladka Kukurice

Fern Fackler is a member of the board of directors of the Czech Fine Arts Foundation, the group that manages the business of the Czech Museum in Cedar Rapids, Iowa. Leona Netolicky Kaplan submitted an alternate method of preparation.

"This recipe has been enjoyed by members of our family and the Netolicky family for many years. When cream was readily available, the first recipe was used. Now when we are more apt to have butter or margarine on hand, the second is easier to use. Our children have always loved this popcorn and delight in experimenting with coloring the syrup–sometimes purple, gray, and colors that are indescribable! We always make it at Christmas time and color some red and some green. We often used pastel colored sweet popcorn in May baskets. Although there is no popcorn in Czechoslovakia, this recipe is 75 years old."

Method 1:

1/2 cup cream
1 cup sugar
4 quarts popcorn

Bring cream and sugar to a boil and simmer for 3 to 5 minutes. Add food coloring if desired. Pour over 4 quarts unsalted popped corn and mix.

Method 2:

3 Tbs. butter or margarine
3 Tbs. water
1 cup sugar
4 quarts popcorn

Bring butter, water, and sugar to a boil and simmer for 3 minutes. Add food coloring if desired. Pour over popped corn and mix.

Homemade Wine
Domací Vino

Evelyn Rainosek Vacera of Bellaire, Texas, grew up by the Colorado River in La Grange, Texas, living on the farm of her grandparents, John and Frances Stolar Svreck. "My uncles would go to the river and pick the grapes when they were ripe and make this wine. I use it for cooking most of the time."

8 cups grapes
4 cups sugar
1 gallon boiling water

Take a clean 1 gallon glass jar with a good lid. Use wild, ripe grapes, or grapes you have in your area. Wash well; fill jar with grapes and sugar. Add boiling water to within 1 inch of the top. Tighten lid and leave to ferment till grape seeds, skins, etc. drop to the bottom. Then it is ready.

Homemade Lye Soap
Domací Mýdlo

Evelyn Rainosek Vacera, Bellaire, Texas, says, "My mother Elizabeth Svrcek Rainosek is in her 70s but she will not have an automatic washing machine. She likes her wringer type, where she can use her homemade soap to wash clothes. When I was growing up in the country, we did not buy shampoo, but used homemade soap. I think we had lots less skin problems than nowadays."

1 can lye
2 1/2 pints cold water
6 pounds clean fat–such as bacon grease, but must not be burned

Slowly add lye to cold water, stir until dissolved. Never use glass, stoneware, or aluminum vessels, Melt fat, let cool to lukewarm. Pour lye solution into melted fat in a thin steady stream while steadily stirring. Takes about 10 to 20 minutes. It will become thick as honey. Pour this into a cardboard box. Let stand 24 hours. Remove and cut into bars. Keep in a cool, dry place.

Listing of Recipes

MEATS AND MAIN DISHES
Marinated Beef 98
Czech Rolled Beef 98
Easter Loaf 99
Boiled Beef with
 Dill Pickle Gravy 99
Veal Ragout with
 Caraway Seeds 99
Pork Roast 100
Spareribs and Potatoes 100
Sauerkraut and Spareribs 100
European Style Paprikas 100
Butchering the Hog and Making
 Sausages 101
Czech Sausage 101
Blood Sausage 101
Pork Sausage 102
Pork Goulash 102
Wenceslaus Square Goulash 102
Pickled Pork Loaf 103
Heart in Sour Cream Gravy 103
Rabbit Meat Loaf 103
Rabbit with Prune Gravy 104
Pickled Fish 104
Poultry Dressing 104
Roast Goose or Duck 105
Roast Duck 105
Chicken Paprika 105
Savoy Cabbage Deluxe 106
Savoy Cabbage and Beef 106
Czech Ham, Cabbage and
 Noodle Casserole 107
Baked Ham and Noodles 107
Black Barley Dish 107

SOUPS AND STEWS
Knuckle Bone Soup 108
Heart Soup 108
Milk Soup 108
Liver Dumpling Soup 109
Old Fashioned Bean Soup 109
Mushroom and Barley Soup 109
Good Nutrition Soup 110
Sauerkraut Soup 110
Mother Vondracek's
 Tomato Soup 110
Garlic Soup 110
Potato Soup with Mushrooms ...111
Potato Soup 111
Cream of Potato and
 Onion Soup 111
Mother's Browned Potato Soup .112
Czech Dill Soup 112
Mother's Potato Goulash 112
Omelette in Milk 112

MUSHROOMS, CABBAGE AND POTATOES
Morel Mushrooms with
 Beef Sauce 113
Hot Mushroom Sandwiches 113
Mushrooms with Cheese 113
Pickled Mushrooms 113
Mushroom Loaf 114
Cabbage Rolls 114
Cabbage Cakes 114
Noodles and Cabbage 115
Konecny's Cabbage Salad 115
Cabbage with
 Caraway Seed Butter 115
Czech Sauerkraut 115
Homemade Sauerkraut 116
Potato Pie 116
Potato Mush 116
Caraway Potatoes 116

NOODLES AND DUMPLINGS
Homemade Noodles 117
Noodles 117
Drop Noodles for Soup 117
Liver Dumplings 117
Farina Puff 118
Bread Dumplings 118

Never Fail Toast Dumplings 118
Grandmother's Baking Powder
  Dumplings 119
Cream of Wheat Dumplings 119
Potato Dumplings 119
Potato Dumplings (with cabbage) .120
Dumplings .120
My Mother's Fruit Dumplings . . .121
Plum Dumplings 121
Prune Dumplings 121

YEAST BREADS
Bohemian Rye Bread 122
Old-Fashioned White Bread 122
Bread Sticks 123
Featherweight Pancakes 123
Grandma Kubicek's Houska 123
Czech Coffee Cake 124
Bohemian Christmas Houska 124
Christmas Sweet Braids 125
Easter Yeast Cake 125

KOLACHES
Kolaches 126
Kolache Dainties 126
Kolaches 127
  Fillings and Toppings
    Crumb Topping 127
    Cherry Filling 127
    Poppy Seed Filling 127
Scones 128
  Fillings and Toppings
    Poppy Seed Filling 128
    Prune Filling 128
    Nut Filling 128
    Cottage Cheese Filling 128
    Streusel Topping 128

DESSERTS
Poppy Seed Cake (buttermilk) 129
Poppy Seed Cake 129
Poppy Seed Coffee Cake 129
Christmas Poppy Seed Cake 130
  Poppy Seed Filling 130

Nut Coffee Cake 130
  Nut Filling 130
Bessie's Apple Strudel 131
Angel Pie 131
Great Grandma Kubicek's
  Rhubarb Custard Pie 132
Nice and Easy Nut Roll 132
  Nut Filling 132
Apple Bublanina 132
Cherry Bublanina 132
Divine Crullers 133
Celestial Crusts 133
Divine Crullers (with cream) 133
Cream Puffs and Filling 134
Mother's Chocolate Fudge 134
Christmas Pudding Candy 135
Czech Garnets 135
Apple Fritters 135
Czechoslovakian Sugar Cookies . .135
Czechoslovakian Cut-Out
  Cookies .136
Molasses-Ginger Bars 136

AND MORE
Cottage Cheese 137
Dill Gravy .137
Tomato Gravy 137
Cream Sauce 138
Mushroom Fritters 138
Sauerkraut Crackers 138
Crackling Crackers 138
Sweet Popcorn 139
Homemade Wine 139
Homemade Lye Soap 139

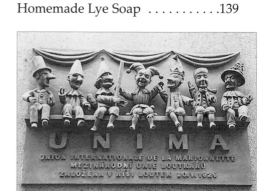

Clock Towers in the Czech Republic

Above: Church of St. Nicholas, left, and St. Vitus Cathedral in Prague
Below, from left, Church of St. Wenceslas, Český Krumlov; České Budějovice, and Tábor

Prague Castle Gate

A Recipe for Life

Success in life is knowing how to
laugh, learn and love.
If you have the affection of others and respect for yourself,
you have true wealth.
If you can take criticism and
dispense tolerance,
you will enrich everyone.

—*Rose Cincara, Cedar Rapids, Iowa*